Structured English Immersion

Structured English Immersion

A Step-by-Step Guide for K–6 Teachers and Administrators

Johanna J. Haver

CORWIN PRESS, INC.
A Sage Publications Company
Thousand Oaks, California

For information:

Corwin Press, Inc.
A Sage Publications Company
2455 Teller Road
Thousand Oaks, California 91320
www.corwinpress.com

Sage Publications Ltd.
6 Bonhill Street
London EC2A 4PU
United Kingdom

Sage Publications India Pvt. Ltd.
B-42 Panchsheel Enclave
Post Box 4109
New Delhi 110 017 India

Printed in the United States of America

Library of Congress Cataloging-in-Publication Data

Haver, Johanna J.
Structured English immersion: A step-by-step guide for K–6 teachers and administrators / Johanna J. Haver.
     p. cm.
Includes bibliographical references and index.
ISBN 0-7619-4567-9 (C) — ISBN 0-7619-4568-7 (P)
     1. English language—Study and teaching (Elementary) 2. English language—Study and teaching—Immersion method. I. Title.
LB1576 .H324 2003
372.6—dc21

                    2002011587

This book is printed on acid-free paper.

02 03 04 05 06 10 9 8 7 6 5 4 3 2 1

Editor-at-Large:	Mark Goldberg
Acquisitions Editor:	Rachel Livsey
Editorial Assistant:	Phyllis Cappello
Copy Editor:	Annette Pagliaro
Production Editor:	Diane S. Foster
Typesetter:	C&M Digitals (P) Ltd
Proofreader:	Scott Oney
Indexer:	Teri Greenberg
Cover Designer:	Tracy E. Miller
Production Artist:	Janet Foulger

Contents

Preface

More and more U.S. public schools are faced with the challenge of educating children who qualify according to federal guidelines for extra help in learning the English language. This student group has come to include not only immigrant children who speak little or no English, but also English-speaking children born in the United States to immigrants. According to interpretations of federal law by the Office for Civil Rights (OCR) in the U.S. Department of Education, any child from a household where a language other than English is spoken can be designated limited English proficient (LEP), as long as the child scores approximately 10% below the mean score for that child's grade level in English proficiency, reading, and/or writing.

LEP NUMBERS ON THE INCREASE

The total number of LEP students in Grades K–12 reached 4,148,997 for the school year 1999–2000. Spanish speakers made up 73%; Vietnamese, at 4%, were the next largest group. The remaining 23% were distributed among more than 100 ethnic and language groups. There was an increase of 104.3% of LEP students since the 1989–1990 school year, compared with a 13.6% increase of all public school students for the same period ("Rural Districts Struggle," 2000).

The largest number of LEP students live in California, followed by Texas, New York, Florida, and Illinois. Other states with large numbers of these children include Massachusetts,

Michigan, New Jersey, Washington, Oregon, Colorado, Idaho, New Mexico, and Arizona. According to the U.S. Education Department, the LEP student population has increased in such states as Arkansas, Nevada, North Carolina, Georgia, Nebraska, Missouri, and Utah ("Rural Districts Struggle," 2000).

The Hispanic population, the group that constitutes the largest percentage of LEP students, has more than doubled in the 1990s. By 2015, Hispanics are projected to become the largest minority group in the United States; by 2025, Hispanics are expected to constitute 25% of students in Grades K–8 and 23% of high school students, according to the U.S. Census Bureau ("Federal Gov't Must Do More," 2000).

THE ACHIEVEMENT GAP

Both local and federal funding have increased substantially for LEP instruction since 1991–1992—when it was estimated at nearly $10 billion (Amselle, 1996, p. 118). Nevertheless, the achievement gains of the largest group, the Hispanics, have been only minimal according to the U.S. Department of Education, as assessed by the National Assessment of Educational Progress (NAEP). Over the past 20 years, the gap in mathematics scores between whites and Hispanic students decreased insignificantly, whereas the gap in reading scores remained the same. The dropout rate for Hispanics has fluctuated between 25% and 35% from 1972 to 1997. In 1998, 30% of Hispanic 16- to 24-year-olds were dropouts, versus 14% of blacks and 8% of whites ("Federal Gov't Must Do More," 2000).

STATE INITIATIVES ABOLISH BILINGUAL EDUCATION

The passing of California's Proposition 227 in 1998, known as the English for the Children initiative, and Proposition 203 in 2000, known as the English for the Children–Arizona initiative, has brought about changes in how the children in these states are to be taught. The initiatives mandate schools to end their bilingual programs and, instead, to offer structured English immersion (SEI) classes "during a temporary transition period not normally intended to exceed one year" (Proposition 203, 2000, p. 150). Polls taken throughout the United States show that the citizens of other states would support similar initiatives.

Two years after the passing of California's Proposition 227, reports appeared in several leading newspapers that LEP students had improved in all subjects due to the elimination of bilingual education and the implementation of structured immersion in California's public schools. A front page *New York Times* article announced that the standardized average test scores of second-grade California LEP students increased from the 19th to the 28th percentile in reading and from the 27th to the 41st percentile in math (Steinberg, 2000). "Two Years of Success: An Analysis of California Test Scores After Proposition 227," completed by the Institute for Research in English Acquisition and Development (READ), concludes that the greatest gains were made in school districts that chose the strictest interpretation of the initiative and implemented the most intensive English-immersion programs (Amselle & Allison, 2000).

Although LEP students in all grade levels showed improvement, the younger students seem to have benefited most from English immersion. This corresponds to the results reached by Johns Hopkins University linguists (Brownlee, 1998). After 25 years of studying the linguistic skills of infants, the experts came to the conclusion that there exists a window of opportunity—until the age of 6—for children to learn a second language easily; after age 6, the ability diminishes with each passing year. According to this report, it makes sense to immerse LEP children in English as early as possible.

The bilingual education advocates interpret the data differently. They believe that other California school reforms such as smaller class size and changes in reading instruction have been responsible for the rise in test scores. They also insist that students will not maintain these academic gains as they progress through the grades.

My Own Experience

As someone who became an English as a second language (ESL) teacher in an inner-city high school after many years of teaching foreign language, I found myself in disagreement with how I was encouraged to teach new English learners, officially referred to as limited English proficient (LEP) students. The accepted methodology of the mid-1980s appeared too unstructured to me. Also, as bilingual education was introduced into my high school, it became increasingly difficult to teach the LEP students enough English to make it possible for them to attend college or obtain jobs of their choice after high school.

At the time, University of California College of Education Professor Stephen Krashen's theory that children should learn "naturally" had gained wide acceptance among English language educators. In their book *The Natural Approach*, Krashen and Terrell maintain that language acquisition does not result from grammar drill, repetition of patterns, or from listening to incomprehensible speech, but develops "naturally" through free conversation (Crawford, 1997). Furthermore, it has been the opinion of Krashen and Terrell that error correction and a student's awareness of grammar rules can inhibit the student's oral language production. For these reasons, they recommend that teachers not engage in the explicit teaching of grammar and the correcting of student errors (Krashen & Terrell, 2000).

Whereas I agree with Krashen and Terrell's opinion that LEP children need opportunities to express themselves in English without being subjected to frequent corrections of errors, my experience has been that they can also be taught the basic structure of the language systematically from the beginning in ways that are both enjoyable and helpful. While a classroom ESL teacher, I developed my own system for teaching prepositions, subject–verb agreement, and verb tense. At the same time, I offered my students many opportunities to speak and write freely. They came to understand that certain lessons dealt with "correctness," whereas other lessons were less restrictive and emphasized the conveying of information. Very gradually, students incorporated the elements of the grammar they had mastered into their free speech and writing.

During the summer of 1999, I had the opportunity to do research at Stanford University. At that point, much of what I had read concerning second language acquisition programs, whether supportive of immersion or bilingual education methodology, had made reference to elementary schools in Canada—where English-dominant children were immersed in French. At the Stanford University libraries, I was able to explore the most recent books and journals written by researchers on that subject. A listing that includes the most significant of these works is found in Recommended Reading for Practitioners at the end of this book.

I discovered that many Canadian immersion authorities are in agreement with me that students need explicit grammar instruction from early on. In a paper from the 6th Nordic Conference on Bilingualism, Diane Larsen-Freeman quotes several researchers who, after examining the Canadian models, had come to the conclusion that grammar is not acquired naturally and does have to be taught. One researcher summed up a consensus opinion that the English-dominant students in Canada who had learned French "naturally" had become "dysfunctional bilinguals who could convey messages but did so very ungrammatically" (1995).

Since that time, the Canadian immersion educators have emphasized the improvement of children's oral and written grammar. They have found that even second graders can learn some basic grammatical structures. According to "Grammar in Grade 2: A Response to Collier," "Experimental studies conducted in French immersion classrooms at Grades 4 to 8 have demonstrated that (a) grammar-oriented tasks in a second language do not have to be dry and dull, and (b) grammar instruction can help to promote lasting improvement in second language proficiency" (Harley, Howard, & Hart, 1998). In an article about French immersion programs in British Columbia, Researchers Elaine Day and Stan Shapson conclude (1996) that students' overall oral and written grammatical skills can be considerably improved and long-lasting if their instruction integrates the systematic instruction of grammar, especially verb tense, with interactive communicative approaches.

A recent *Canadian Modern Language Review* article, "Comprehension-Based Learning: The Limits of 'Do It Yourself,'" compares two eighth-grade groups of students who were taught ESL for 6 years in highly communicative school environments. The only difference between the two groups was that one group was taught with little or no focus on form, whereas the other group received form-focused instruction and feedback on error correction regularly. Whereas both groups performed at equal levels in comprehension and some measures of oral production, the group with instruction that included focus on form, such as verb tense and use of the pronoun, did considerably better in writing and some levels of oral production (Lightbown, Halter, White, & Horst, 2002).

Rationale for Structured English Immersion

Total immersion into the mainstream from the beginning, often referred to as "submersion," can work for some very young children. However, without specific instruction, the LEP children are likely to become confused and overwhelmed at being exposed to a variety of contradictory English speech patterns. It is unreasonable to expect new learners of English to be able to distinguish English slang, dialect, and improper grammar from the accepted Standard American English (SAE) on their own.

LEP students respond well to a plan of instruction in which each aspect of the language builds on another, with plenty of opportunities for practice. It is similar to learning to play the piano. Hitting the keys is part of the process, but to just pound on the piano without any concern as to how the notes and chords relate to each other is not going to create beautiful music.

SEI offers LEP children an ideal format. The goal is for these children to gain fluency in English as quickly as possible in a nonthreatening setting and to move gradually into the mainstream, the place where the challenging classes abound, and learn with the other children.

SEI differs from typical ESL methodology in that it discourages the use of the native language and provides a more structured approach to learning English. Also, SEI blends English grammar and vocabulary instruction with the teaching of content, a system that may or not be part of an ESL curriculum. SEI and ESL methodology share common elements such as an emphasis on developing listening skills first, hands-on activities, and student dramatizations.

OVERVIEW OF CHAPTERS

The suggestions in the chapters of this book are based on my own 32 years of teaching experience, research, and interviews with several successful educators. The focus is on Grades K–6, although many ideas can be adapted for Grades 7–12. The purpose is to provide concrete ideas and practical class-room examples for teachers and administrators who want to use SEI methodology. It is meant to be especially helpful to the rapidly increasing number of educators who are required by law or inclination to shift to SEI but do not have enough information or practical materials to feel comfortable doing so.

Throughout the book, names are given to teachers and students. These names are fictitious, created solely to better explain strategies.

Chapter 1 presents the initial steps necessary for setting up SEI in a school. It takes the reader through the process of identifying, testing, and then placing LEP students either into SEI classes or into the mainstream as transitional students. This chapter is of particular interest to administrators; however, teachers' awareness of this process is important in case they have questions concerning the placement of students.

Chapter 2 offers teachers listening strategies that are basic to mastering English. It begins with techniques for students who do not understand English and gradually leads up to techniques that can be used in mainstream classes where LEP students have been transitioned.

Chapter 3 begins with a general depiction of SEI 1. It then elaborates on how the SEI 2 and 3 teachers can incorporate various mainstream content curricula into their instruction.

Chapter 4 separates SEI 1 from SEI 2 and 3 in description and linguistic elements to be covered. It details a format for moving students through SEI in such a way that they gain all the basic information that they will need to get along, with assistance, in the mainstream within the approximate time period of a year.

Chapter 5 provides mainstream teachers with ways to assist those students who are still in SEI classes for some of the day or have recently transitioned entirely from SEI instruction into the mainstream.

Chapter 6 elaborates on how school policies in general can best serve the LEP students. This includes ideas on scheduling, involving parents, attendance, alignment of curricula, and native/foreign language instruction.

Chapter 7 consists of an overview of the previous chapters in the form of outlines of the material in each previous chapter and two flowcharts. The first flowchart shows how students can be placed according to their scores on either of the two major English language oral proficiency tests. The second one depicts the sequences from SEI 1 to full mainstreaming.

Resource A, Recommended Reading for Practitioners, is meant to assist those teachers who want to continue to learn how to implement SEI and/or are interested in the research on immersion education. Resource B lists 15 schools in six states where teachers use SEI methodology to instruct LEP students. Initially, the list comprised about 100 schools. Through telephone conversations, e-mail communications, and further discussions with professional educators, I shortened that list to 15 schools that I could recommend heartily.

I learned about the Arizona and Pennsylvania school programs through my work as a READ Institute writer and researcher of the Arizona Department of Education English Language Acquisition Program Cost Study. Kevin Clark's (2000) study on how five California Districts switched from bilingual education to SEI instruction led me to the Atwater Elementary, Orange Unified, and Riverdale Unified School Districts. *No Excuses: Lessons From 21 High-Performing, High-Poverty Schools* (Carter, 2000), a book that features 21 high-performing, high-poverty schools, provided me information about Bennett-Kew Elementary School in California, KIPP Academy in Texas, and Portland Elementary School in Arkansas. Reliable professional educators recommended 3D Academy, Kelso Elementary School, and Oceanside Unified Elementary School District to me. An Education Testing Service (ETS) and Education Commission of the States (ECS) conference that I attended in the fall of 2001 featured Dover Elementary School in Dover, Florida.

ACKNOWLEDGMENTS

This book would not exist if it were not for Mark Goldberg, Senior Editor of Corwin Press, and Jorge Amselle, former Executive Director of the READ Institute. Mark Goldberg responded enthusiastically when I informed him that I wanted to write a book about structured English immersion. With patience, persistence, and exceptional skill as an author himself, he took me down the book-writing path that has led to publication. Jorge Amselle answered my questions concerning SEI with prompt e-mail responses and then made it possible for me to work as a READ Institute writer of the Arizona Department of Education Cost Study of English Language Acquisition Programs. In this position, I was able to gain access to all aspects of SEI instruction.

This book has been influenced by several excellent foreign language teachers, too many to name individually, who have instructed me in Latin, German, Spanish, and French over a span of more than 40 years. I am especially grateful to the German instructors at the 1967 National Defense Education Act Institute at Montana State University in Bozeman, Montana, who took me through the process of learning and teaching German through immersion methodology. Without that experience, I would have left the profession of teaching early on and would not have become fluent in German.

Four school administrators deserve recognition for proving to me that LEP students can reach high levels of achievement if they are provided with the right school environment. They include Dr. Frances Amabisca, former superintendent of Avondale Elementary Schools in Avondale, Arizona; Dr. Greg Riccio, former principal of Central High School in Phoenix, Arizona; Dr. Carol Peck, superintendent of Alhambra Elementary School District in Phoenix, Arizona; and Margaret Garcia-Dugan, principal of Glendale High School in Glendale, Arizona.

Two individuals whose ideas are incorporated to a large degree into this book's teacher strategies are Tad Takahashi, former Supervisor of English Instruction in the public schools of Himeji, Japan; and Karen Henderson, English as a Second Language District Coordinator of Glendale Union High School District in Glendale, Arizona. Mr. Takahashi, a Japanese researcher of Total Physical Response (TPR) methodology, broadened my understanding of how TPR could be applied to all levels of English language instruction. Karen Henderson shared with me her vast knowledge of strategies that work well for LEP students in mainstream classes.

The colleagues who have influenced me through the years are too many to name. However, the following educators deserve special recognition because they contributed ideas concerning strategies, curriculum, and/or organization of SEI levels to this book:

- Vanessa Dehne, retired high school teacher and department chair of reading and ESL in Phoenix, Arizona
- Ron Dixon, Alhambra Elementary School District Assistant Superintendent for Academic Services in Phoenix, Arizona
- Pat Doran, literacy consultant and retired former elementary teacher in Phoenix, Arizona
- Charles Garcia, retired high school teacher and department chair of foreign language and ESL in Phoenix, Arizona
- Linda Garcia, elementary teacher in Phoenix, Arizona
- JoAnn Lawson, retired high school teacher and department chair of English and ESL in Phoenix, Arizona
- Ann Marie Renaud, elementary district reading specialist and consultant in Hailey, Idaho

Corwin Press Acquisitions Editor Rachel Livsey and three practitioner reviewers helped me enormously with the tedious job of preparing the final draft. Their practical and intelligent suggestions have made it possible for me to make many worthwhile improvements in organization and content.

My special friend, Lloyd Engel, deserves recognition for listening to me and encouraging me to keep to the task through the many months that it has taken to write this book.

The contributions of the following reviewers are gratefully acknowledged:

Arlene Myslinski
ESL/Business Teacher
Buffalo Grove High School
Buffalo Grove, IL

Pauline Schara, Ed.D.
    Principal
    Yorba Linda, CA

Nancy Law, Ph.D.
    Consultant
    Retired Research & Evaluation Director
    Sacramento City Schools
    Sacramento, CA

This book is dedicated to my many former
students from whom I gained immeasurable joy

**CORWIN
PRESS**

The Corwin Press logo—a raven striding across an open book—
represents the happy union of courage and learning. We are a
professional-level publisher of books and journals for K-12 educators,
and we are committed to creating and providing resources that
embody these qualities. Corwin's motto is "Success for All Learners."

About
the Author

Johanna J. Haver is a retired teacher with 32 years of classroom experience. She began in 1966 as a teacher of German and Latin at a high school in Casper, Wyoming. Eight years later, she developed and supervised a remedial reading program for elementary students, many of them identified as limited English proficient (LEP), in the farm community of Avondale, Arizona. She spent the last 18 years of her career in a Phoenix high school district where she taught German, Latin, reading, and, eventually, English as a second language (ESL).

She has taught in both the German and Japanese school systems. During the 1970–1971 school year, she taught English as a foreign language to elementary-age German *Gymnasium* students in Essen-Steele, West Germany. As Phoenix Sister City Teacher to Himeji, Japan, she taught English conversation to Japanese high school students from 1987–1989.

Since retirement in 1999, she has become an independent education writer and researcher. In March of 2001, she was commissioned by the Institute for English Acquisition and Development (READ Institute) in Washington, D.C., to write extensive reviews of the English language acquisition programs in five model Arizona schools. These reviews were incorporated into the 2001 Arizona Department of Education Cost Study of English Language Acquisition Programs. Also, from 2000–2001, she served as a member of Arizona Department of Education task forces for which the goal was to advise the Arizona superintendent of instruction on the implementation of English language acquisition programs.

She earned a B.A. in German from the University of Wyoming and an M.A. in German from the University of Arizona. She became certified as a reading specialist and ESL teacher through postgraduate study at Arizona State University.

She may be reached at the following addresses:

j.haver@worldnet.att.net

http://home.att.net/~j.haver/

1

Identification, Assessment, and Placement

Structured English immersion (SEI) is based on the theory that children learn a second language best when they are integrated with other children who speak that language with native-speaker ability. The beginning English language learners are separated initially—for as short a time as possible—from the other children, to receive English and content-area instruction systematically in a nonthreatening setting. However, even at that beginning stage, these children participate in the mainstream classes in which language is not necessary for success: hands-on science, music, art, and physical education, for instance.

CALIFORNIA SCHOOL DISTRICTS IMPLEMENT SEI

Kevin Clark, a consultant and educator specializing in the implementation of effective programs for second language learners, outlines a format that has been used in several California schools. Non-English-speaking children progress through three stages as beginners until they can be transitioned to an intermediate level where they are mainstreamed gradually into the regular classes. When a student reaches the fluent English proficient (FEP) level, he or she no longer receives special instruction in the area of English language acquisition. However, in the mainstream classes, the limited English proficient (LEP) students continue to be helped by means of specially designed academic instruction (SDAI) until all skills are on a par with those of the other children (Clark, 2000).

SDAI refers to the classroom use of tools that facilitate learning for LEP children in particular. These include visuals that make identification of specific items immediate and processes that facilitate learning for all children. The strategies suggested in Chapter 5 of this book would qualify as SDAI.

Literacy Problems

SEI differs dramatically from many English as a second language (ESL) programs in that students are not kept out of the mainstream due to literacy problems. Too frequently, ESL students have become stuck at particular levels due to poor reading and writing skills. As a result, such children remain in ESL classes for years. They continue to practice what they had mastered and receive little help on the particular literacy skills that they lack.

The theory behind holding students back due to poor literacy skills has been that students identified as LEP must be taught reading and writing together in ways different from those of other students. However, according to a report by Jill Fitzgerald (1995, p. 184) on the cognitive processes of LEP students, there is no evidence that LEP children need notably divergent forms of instruction for this. When a child has literacy problems, the best remedy should have greater weight than the particular "label" assigned to that student. For instance, some LEP students may have difficulty reading multisyllable words but surpass the other LEP students in oral language development. It makes sense to give these students the particular help they need while maintaining them as much as possible in regular classes.

Assessment Is Crucial

Assessment begins on the first day of school when students come to register. All parents fill out a primary language survey that provides general information about the children's language or languages. From that data the students most likely in need of help in English are identified and then administered an English oral language proficiency examination. The students who score less than proficient in English are then administered a similar test in their primary language, as is commonly mandated by state law.

During the first weeks of school, teachers are encouraged to refer for testing students who seem to have difficulty with communication. Possibly, some prospective LEP children were not identified correctly on the primary language survey because their parents either did not fill out the survey or did not complete it properly. Other explanations should also be considered. For instance, the difficulty could be the result of physical, mental, or emotional handicaps that other school programs address. It must be kept in mind that the purpose of the English language proficiency assessment is to properly place students who cannot do regular schoolwork because their dominant language is not English.

Teachers and other staff members are instructed to look for specific behaviors that may identify a child as LEP:

1. The child does not respond appropriately when spoken to.

2. The child does not know the vocabulary of his or her peers.

3. The child is difficult to understand.

4. The grammatical errors of the child are atypical of children of the same age.

The person who notices the behavior notes the specifics and sends the information to the person in charge of the assessments. The student in question is evaluated as soon as possible by properly trained personnel. The objectives here are to determine with as much precision as possible what is the matter and what form help should take.

The Primary Home Language Survey

The Office for Civil Rights (OCR) in the U.S. Department of Education requires schools to ask questions that have to do solely with the home languages of the individual students. If a parent gives a single affirmative answer to whether the child learned to speak a language other than English first, whether the child currently speaks a language other than English, or whether a language other than English is spoken in the home, the child is classified as primary home language other than English (PHLOTE). Whereas such information is helpful, inquiring exclusively about home languages can be misleading. For instance, the child may have spent only his or her infancy in a foreign country, foreign-born grandparents may be living in the home, or perhaps members of the family are learning a foreign language together. Such situations may not have a negative impact on a child's ability to speak English and should not lead to a child being placed in a program for LEP children.

Too many cases each year are reported of parents who have angrily pulled their children out of bilingual or ESL programs. Each child had been identified incorrectly as LEP because of a check mark or an answer on a form, but the child's English was quite appropriate for his or her age. Such encounters result in a loss of trust between parents and school, not to mention the problems caused to the children.

For proper placement, the survey should include questions about the child's ability to speak English. The following questions would be reasonable in a primary home language survey:

1. What language or languages are spoken in your child's home?

2. What language or languages does your child speak?

3. In what language does your child have the most fluency?

4. Do you believe that your child needs help in learning English?

If at all possible, the survey should be written in the languages most likely spoken by the parents at the particular school. People who know these languages should be available to present and explain the survey. Each parent's written language of preference can be noted according to the language of the survey that the parent chooses to fill out. Because the relationship between parent and school is important, it would be a courtesy to send information to the parent(s) or guardian(s) of each child in their language of choice whenever possible.

1. What language or languages are spoken in your child's home? If the survey indicates that a language other than English is spoken in the home, the child need not be administered oral language proficiency tests unless the next question indicates that the child does not know English. The response should simply be recorded as data that could lead to the development of foreign language or cultural programs that may interest the child.

2. What language or languages does your child speak? If the response states that the child speaks English in addition to another language, it should be recorded as data for reference concerning the implementation of foreign language and/or cultural programs. There is no need to administer oral language proficiency tests to this child. However, if it is indicated that the child does not speak English, the child should be administered the tests in English and the native language.

3. In what language does your child have the most fluency? If the child's dominant language is identified as other than English, the child should first be administered an oral English language proficiency test and then one in the native language. It seems likely, but not certain, that this child will qualify as an LEP student. However, it is possible for a child whose dominant language is not English, but who has been immersed in an English-speaking environment, such as a nursery school or the homes of English-only neighbors, to have gained near-native English ability and yet to have greater proficiency in the first language.

4. Do you believe that your child needs help in learning English? The parents who answer "yes" to this question will most likely support the placement of their children in SEI or transitional English language classes, those classes in the mainstream that provide special adaptations for LEP students. It is likely, but not an absolute, that these children are the ones most in need of help with English. They should take the oral English and primary language proficiency tests as soon as possible so that their placement is immediate.

The Oral Language Proficiency Test

The students identified as possible LEP students due to the responses on the primary language survey and/or teacher/staff recommendations take the oral portion of the English language proficiency test. Sometimes this can be done at the time of registration; otherwise, a time should be scheduled before classes start or, if this is difficult, as soon as possible. It is best to begin with the students most likely to need help, the students recommended on the survey.

Most school districts use widely respected, commercially developed oral language proficiency tests such as the IDEA Proficiency Test (IPT) by Ballard & Tighe or the Language Assessment Scales (LAS) by CTB McGraw-Hill. Both tests are explained later in this chapter. However, some districts develop their own tests, a process not recommended because such tests have questionable reliability and validity. California has mandated that all school districts use the California English Language Development Test (CELDT), an adaptation of the LAS test. Arizona requires that districts choose among the IPT, the LAS, and two other English proficiency tests.

Standardizing the process in a state makes sense because such information can then be transferred to and understood by the various districts. In addition, keeping track of the progress of LEP students through a standardized process can be streamlined to such a degree that weaknesses in programs can be quickly discovered and remedied. A trained person must administer the oral part of the English proficiency test one-to-one. The two other portions that deal with reading and writing skills can be given later in a class setting. The publishers of the tests provide interpretations of the scores that can then be used for designation and classification purposes.

The commercial oral language proficiency tests have limitations. For example, the test scores are based on norms that identify students whose English language ability is less than that of the average native speakers of the same age. This means that many children who speak only English could be identified as LEP. Also, a preoccupied, timid, or inhibited child may not demonstrate his true oral language ability. For these reasons, the test results should be considered only approximations, and teachers should always be alert to recommend more or less help when they come to know more about a child's ability. In some cases, a child should even be retested after he or she gains confidence.

The problem of incorrect identification is less feasible if the initial language survey asks specific questions about the child's language(s) rather than general questions about the home language(s). Also, it is likely that students fluent in English would be quickly spotted in an SEI classroom of children who speak little or no English. For a transitional program, false identification would not be a problem because the child would already be placed in a mainstream class.

Commercial oral language proficiency tests can be helpful if used with an understanding of their limitations and purpose. They offer a starting point upon which a teacher can develop instruction. The publishers of leading oral language proficiency tests agree that certain conditions should be met concerning the actual administration of the test:

1. The administrator's voice, diction, and tone should be pleasant to listen to and easy to understand.

2. The surroundings should have no visual and/or auditory distractions.

3. The examiner's table or desk should have only testing materials on it.

4. The temperature should be comfortable.

5. The setting should be private, away from other students and adults.

6. The time should be reasonable, not right before lunch, recess, or school dismissal.

7. The person administering the test should spend a few minutes building rapport with the child.

8. The administer should seek permission from the child to ask questions such as, "May I ask you some questions?" or " Is this a good time for you?" If the child says "no," the test should be rescheduled. However, it should be made clear that the child must take the test within a reasonable time.

Two Representative Tests

The oral sections of the IPT and the LAS share some advantages. Both tests have demonstrated field-tested reliability and validity. They are available in both Spanish and English. The scripted instructions for the tests are easy to follow and the companies provide substantial help with the training of examiners. The scoring for both tests is easy to compute with little room for misinterpretations.

The IPT oral tests for Grades K through 6 and 7 through 12 measure listening comprehension and speaking ability. The test does not ask the student to read or write. It begins with some simple sample questions to put the student at ease. For example, the examiner may ask the student to give his age or grade, point to an object, identify a part of the body, or complete a sentence. The first questions of the actual test are similar, and just as basic, but gradually increase in difficulty. The examiner asks the student to identify objects in pictures, complete sentences, say whether words are the same or different, retell a story, or anticipate what will happen next in a story. At the same time, the examiner has lists of the acceptable responses as well as prompts that he or she can use if the student is hesitant to respond.

At the end of each test section is a scoring grid that tells the examiner to either stop the testing or move on to the next section. The student is not pushed beyond his or her frustration level. The total points fit into categories from Level A (non-English-speaking) to Level F (fluent-English-speaking) according to the particular grade level of the student. Understandably, a fifth or sixth grader would be expected to accumulate more points than a first grader. The graphs at the end of the test booklet explain the process quite well. The oral portion of the IPT can take from 5 to 20 minutes. The higher the oral English proficiency of the student, the longer the time it takes to complete the test.

The LAS oral tests range from PRE-LAS for ages 4 to 6 to A-LAS for adults. Small children ages 5 and 6 respond to pictures on a game board. The test can be administered by means of an audiocassette for those who are concerned about standardization. Students in Grades 1 through 6 take forms 1C and 1D; Grades 7 through 12, forms 2C and 2D. Like the IPT oral tests, the student is not asked to read or write. Each section begins with a practice section. In the first part, the student responds to "Simon Says" requests. The second section solicits responses concerning objects and what they are for. The objects may be utensils, food, or animals. The third part asks the student to repeat sentences after the examiner. The fourth part requires that the student identify objects in pictures. The fifth part asks the student to listen carefully to a story that is accompanied by pictures. The student then retells the story by explaining each picture. At the same time, the examiner records the responses both on an answer sheet and by means of a tape recorder.

Like the IPT oral test, each section offers a grid that tells the examiner to either stop or to go on according to the responses. The examiner keeps track of the student's answers in an answer booklet where the number of correct answers is added up and interpreted. There are examples of correct responses for each section.

The total points range from numerical Level 1 (non-English-speaker) to Levels 4 and 5 (fluent-English-speaker). The examiner can use a short form and/or a long form for scoring. The short form provides a general score for placement; the long form, a breakdown of individual skills. The oral test takes 10 to 15 minutes to administer, but is considerably more complex than the IPT to score. However, the scoring process of the LAS offers more information about the student.

It is important for the schools to look at each test series before making a final judgment. There are many other choices available; however, the IPT and the LAS are the most widely used at the present time.

PROPER PLACEMENT OF STUDENTS

If the student scored less than fluent on the English oral proficiency test, the laws in many states require that an oral test be given in the student's native language as well. The second oral test can be given right after the first one, or later on, and in the format of an interview. Both the IPT and the LAS offer oral language proficiency tests in Spanish. It is likely that native speakers or interpretation services in the community can help with this process. Questions chosen by the school can be recorded in the language by a native speaker and used repeatedly. Special arrangements can be made to interpret the student's recorded responses. Also, immediate interpretation is offered at any time through a service of Monterey Language Line. Contact information for this service can be found at the end of the chapter.

It is important to note that students who score higher on the oral section of the English language proficiency test than the oral test of their native language are not LEP, even if the score in English is less than fluent. Indeed, 41% to 44% of children who speak only English would score less than fluent on this norm-referenced test.

There is always the possibility that something other than another language has interfered with a child's English language development. The child may have a speech impediment, hearing difficulties, an emotional problem, or a learning disability, any of which might inhibit the child's responses to questions. It is up to the school official or school team that has been assigned this responsibility to make a decision after reviewing all the data. That official or team should consider every piece of pertinent information concerning the student.

Test Scores Are Limited Gauges

The placement of students must allow for flexibility because, as stated before, the test scores are only approximations. Boston University professor Christine Rossell (1999) maintains that the research indicates that teachers are much better than tests in determining whether a child is proficient in English. However, oral proficiency tests remain an adequate first screening; the law generally requires decisions that can be documented.

Students whose scores fall in the range of nonspeaker of English on the oral part of the English language proficiency test should be placed, most likely, at SEI Level 1. On the IPT, this would be Level A for kindergarten students and Levels A or B for children in Grades 1 through 6; on the LAS, Level 1. Level C on the IPT and Level 2 on the LAS would indicate placement in SEI Level 2 for students in Grades 2 and 3 and SEI Level 3 for students in Grades 4 through 6. Students who score higher than those scores, but not yet at levels designated as fluent according to the tests' publishers, should be considered "transitional," which means that they should be mainstreamed, but provided with additional assistance.

To be designated fluent speakers and not LEP, kindergarten students should score at or above Level C on the IPT and Level 4 or above on the LAS; first graders, at or above Level E on the IPT and at or above Level 4 on the LAS; and students in Grades 2 through 6 at Level F on the IPT and Level 4 or 5 on the LAS.

It may turn out, as happens with many native speakers, that these children need extra help with literacy skills. However, like all children, the reason for this is difficult to ascertain. What matters is that every child who lags behind in literacy skills must receive extra help, regardless of whether he or she speaks a language other than English.

COMPLIANCE WITH THE LAW

The Office for Civil Rights (OCR) in the U.S. Department of Education oversees federal programs to ensure that students are receiving proper services. It is not the function of the OCR to decide which programs are offered to LEP students; however, the OCR does have the right to ask for information concerning programs and to expect notification of any major program changes.

Jim Littlejohn, an education equity consultant and a former program director at the U.S. Department of Education OCR, offers the following suggestions to help schools prepare for possible OCR investigations:

1. All involved administrators and teachers should know how their program works, what the law requires, and the OCR policies.

2. The district federal programs director or other appointed official should be prepared to show how the program is in compliance with the law and where the district needs waivers to do more than the OCR requires.

3. Neither administrators nor teachers should be afraid to question OCR demands.

4. Nothing should be promised to the OCR that cannot be delivered.

5. All transactions should be documented.

6. The school should require that the OCR present its findings in writing; no action should be taken until that has occurred.

7. Negotiation between the school and the OCR should be a continuous process.

Federal law expects school programs for LEP students to be based on sound educational theory, to provide LEP students the opportunity to participate with the other students in the educational offerings, and to show evidence of producing academic success. A well-implemented SEI program can measure up to this easily for several reasons:

■ SEI accelerates achievement because it focuses on teaching English to learners from the beginning.
■ Segregation is minimal because the program is designed to mainstream most students within a year.
■ Academic progress is continuous because content-area subjects are taught, even at the beginning level, through sheltered English, a system of using simplified English to explain concepts. (Center for Equal Opportunity, 2000, pp. 36-40)

SELECTED RESOURCES FOR TEACHERS

Oral Language Proficiency Tests

- *Idea Proficiency Test (IPT)* by Ballard & Tighe Publishers: 1-800-321-4332 or www.ballard-tighe.com
- *Language Assessment Scales (LAS)* by CTB/McGraw-Hill: 1-800-538-9547 or www.ctb.com

Translation Service

- *Monterey Language Line:* www.monterey.org/langcap/attll.html

2

Listening Skills

When children, and particularly immigrant children, who do not speak English well—or at all—enroll in our schools, they find themselves immersed in a strange, new world of incomprehensible sounds. They seek out fellow students who speak their language, even if all they have in common is that language. They know that many people consider them to be "different." They are embarrassed when they cannot understand and, consequently, will sometimes pretend to grasp what they cannot. Often they must endure taunts and teasing from their classmates and occasionally impatience from teachers. The older the child is, the more self-conscious he or she becomes, which makes the adjustment even more difficult.

FIRST STEPS: EASING INTO THE NEW LANGUAGE

This chapter will focus on developing the first skill— listening—in structured English immersion (SEI) classes, with some discussion as to how specific strategies can be applied to the mainstream classes into which limited English proficient (LEP) students have transitioned. The goal is to move children to mainstream classes as transitional students as soon as they are ready and then to completely integrate them into the mainstream. The guidelines that follow can facilitate that process.

■ *Practice the Golden Rule.* The teacher should treat the newcomer children with friendliness, genuine interest, and empathy. This can begin with a daily smile and greeting. It is the obligation of the teacher to assure the apprehensive students that everything will work out and to encourage assistance from the other students who have been in the school longer. These newcomers must be allowed plenty of time to accustom themselves to the new language and school routine.

■ *Maintain the proper noise level.* The classroom must be free of as many auditory distractions and problems as possible: poor acoustics, a teacher's voice that does not carry, talkative students, loud machines outside, and the like will interfere with these children's English language development.

■ *Encourage students to speak English.* It is especially disruptive if the children hear phrases in their native language mixed with English from the teacher and/or other students. The children will simply tune out the English and pay attention to their native language, which they can comprehend easily and quickly.

■ *Use native language for quick explanations.* At times it will be necessary for the teacher to make something clear in another language or to call on a child to explain something to another child in a language other than English. Time should never be wasted on long explanations and dramatics to communicate the meaning of a word or phrase when a quick translation is easily available. The native language should be spoken briefly, followed by an immediate return to English.

■ *Alleviate fear.* The teacher must build confidence in these children who most likely fear that they will not be able to master the foreign sounds around them. In the beginning, it is essential that the lessons be set up so that every child succeeds. Such a task is possible, as illustrated in the examples that follow.

Example 1: First Day of SEI Level 1

Mrs. Dahl walks in front of her non-English-speaking students who have been placed in her SEI Level 1 class. She looks at them and smiles. She sits down in a chair, stands up, and says, "I stand up." As she says "I," she points to herself. She sits down and repeats the same action and words. Then, she sits down again. This time she holds out her hands to the students as she rises and says, "Everyone, stand up." Once the students have stood up, she says, "I sit down. Everyone, sit down." She models the actions as few times as possible because her goal is to get the students to respond to her words, not to imitate her actions. She continues the process, adding new commands while repeating the earlier ones frequently and out of sequence:

- "I raise my hand. Raise your hand." (Teacher, then student action)
- "I put my hand down. Put your hand down." (Teacher, then student action)
- "Stand up. Raise your hand." (Student action)
- "Put your hand down. Raise your hand." (Student action)
- "Put your hand down. I raise my foot." (Student, then teacher action)
- "Raise your foot. I put my foot down." (Student, then teacher action)
- "Put your foot down and sit down." (Student action)
- "Put your hand up and stand up." (Student action)
- "Put your hand down and sit down." (Student action)
- "I raise both my hands. Raise both your hands." (Teacher, then student action)

The process continues. The commands become more complex and longer but always with frequent repetitions: "Put your left hand on your right shoulder and stand up." Mrs. Dahl observes all of the students to make sure that her pace is neither too fast nor too slow.

Gradually, the students are able to respond to Mrs. Dahl's words automatically without any hesitation. She continues the routine with the entire class, then half the class, and finally small groups. The students who are not performing are able to practice listening to their teacher's commands while watching their classmates' actions. Finally, she asks for volunteers to respond individually to the commands. If a child errs, she smiles and has a group or the entire class review the commands. Then she lets that same child try again—but only if the child is willing to do so.

After the students have completed many actions correctly, Mrs. Dahl praises the students with "That's right!" "Very good!" or "You can do it!" The children may not understand the words, but will pick up the positive tone in her voice. No one is forced; everyone is allowed plenty of time to listen and respond appropriately.

TIME ON TASK

The time spent on the exercise varies according to the age of the students. In the beginning, students in Grades 2 through 6 spend 15 to 20 minutes on this during any one time period and then work up to 30 minutes within a couple of weeks. Children in kindergarten or first grade can initially spend 10 to 15 minutes on the exercise; this time segment can be gradually extended to 20 to 25 minutes. For children in junior or senior high, 45-minute sessions are reasonable. The time segments for the younger children can be repeated two or three times throughout the day. Of course, there are many variances among student groups; the teacher should not hesitate to adjust the time frame accordingly.

If children do not want to participate, they may simply observe the process until they are ready. Little by little, the entire class will trust the teacher. The students decide that learning English can be fun and certainly not as difficult as originally thought.

TOTAL PHYSICAL RESPONSE

Responding physically to verbal commands is called Total Physical Response (TPR), a methodology developed in the late 1970s by James J. Asher, professor of psychology and former associate dean at San Jose State University. Asher has become well-known for his book about TPR, *Learning Another Language Through Actions*, first published in 1977 and now in its sixth edition. He has also written, directed, and produced video demonstrations that show some practical applications of TPR. After much research and experimentation with control groups, Asher concluded that language learners needed the opportunity to practice listening without being expected to respond verbally. Additionally, he discovered that forcing verbal responses actually slowed down the learning process, whereas soliciting physical responses to verbal requests speeded it up.

KINDERGARTEN AND FIRST-GRADE SEI

Asher's theory fits well with the traditional way that many teachers have run kindergarten and first-grade classes. The students are offered many opportunities to respond physically to commands. Every day the teacher tells the students to sit down, be quiet, take out their crayons, stand up, open the door, close the door, get the folders from the shelves, and so on. These small children are not expected to talk much in the early grades. As a result, they develop their listening ability in a natural way.

Some schools find it is not necessary to teach kindergarten and first-grade LEP students separately. Of course, this will depend on the skills of both the LEP and native-speaking children. If, for example, you have 20 native speakers and 20 students who know little or no English, the students would be separated for at least portions of the day until the SEI program brings the LEP students to the point where they can be fully integrated.

As already explained in the Preface, at the age of 6 and younger, children can learn a new language more easily than at any other age and progress is usually rapid. Many of the suggestions here can be used for very young native speakers because all children should learn basic language skills at these early levels. However, at the same time, the teacher should be aware that some of the new English language learners will need more time to listen to and practice even very basic English. It is advisable to offer these children, along with other children who are not keeping up, an extra hour or more of instructional time that will help bridge the gap.

Example 2: A Personal Story

The German schools put their very young non-German-speaking children right in with the German children at the primary level. I saw how well this works in 1970 when I enrolled my 4-year-old daughter in a kindergarten located in a suburb of Essen, a large industrial city in Germany. At the time, I was teaching at a German *Gymnasium* (university preparatory school). During the first week, my daughter expressed frustration that she could not communicate with the other children. For that reason, she took some American storybooks to school "to teach those German children some English!" However, at the end of the day, she concluded, "Those German children can't learn English!"

When my daughter realized that English would get her nowhere at this school, she learned German rapidly. It made all the difference that she was not expected to talk at first, but simply to do as she was told. When she did speak, she said a few simple German words, then babbled nonsensically in what sounded like German. Gradually her German speech patterns turned into complete sentences. The process was similar to the way she had learned English as an infant, but progressed at a faster pace. Within 9 months she could speak German as well as the German children and without any detectable accent. Basically, her teacher used what has come to be known as TPR as she helped her begin the new language.

Example 3: More TPR—All SEI Levels

Mr. George, who teaches the second level of SEI to second and third graders, takes advantage of opportunities to give students specific instructions: "Omar, go to the metal cabinet, open the third drawer from the top, and take out the file with your name on it." Also, students review by playing games such as "Simon Says," in which the teacher, aide, or student leads the others:

> "Simon says to take four steps forward." (Student action)
>
> "Simon says to put your left hand on your head." (Student action)
>
> "Simon says to take three steps backward." (Student action)
>
> "Take two steps to the right." (Student action)
>
> "Wrong! I didn't say 'Simon Says.'"

Whoever makes a wrong move or acts out a command that does not begin with "Simon Says" is out. The game continues until only one person remains who is then named the winner.

Example 4: TPR With Objects—All SEI Levels

As the students move along in SEI Level 1 and advance into SEI Levels 2 and 3, the teacher introduces many other activities that enable the students to develop listening skills through actions. Students can be asked to draw pictures or identify objects on worksheets or the blackboard in response to specific directions given by the teacher.

■ Students can be asked to manipulate objects. For instance, Mr. George puts a shoebox on a table in front of him for all the students to see. Mr. George talks as he takes objects out of the box and places them in various spots:

"I open the red box and take out a leather wallet."

"I put the lid on the right side of the red box."

"I open the leather wallet and take out five dollars."

"I put the leather wallet on the lid and put the five dollars next to the wallet."

"Now I take a green box out of the red box."

"I open the green box and take out a small doll."

"I put the small doll back into the red box."

"I take a key out of the red box and put it into the green box."

"I put the green box next to the lid of the red box."

■ After manipulating the objects, Mr. George asks a volunteer to come up and respond to his commands. The other students listen and watch because they know that they are expected to learn to understand these commands. He directs the student, "Open the red box. Put the lid on the table next to the red box. Take out the green box. Open the green box. Take out the doll and put the green box on the lid of the red box. Put the doll on top of the green box." He keeps the original vocabulary for the most part, but changes the specific commands with each student.

■ Mr. George continues and helps the students with hints: "Not the red box, the green box!" The students laugh and have a lot of fun with the challenge. This can be made into a game in which a student or team of students competes to see who can respond correctly to the most commands. The rule can be that the student has to sit down as soon as he or she misses a command.

■ To quiz the students on how well they have listened, Mr. George gives them a true-false test. He explains, "Write 'T' if what I say agrees with what I do, or 'F' if it doesn't agree." He proceeds: "I open the red box." He opens the red box and then gives students the time to write "T" or "F." "I take out a green box." He takes out the green box and pauses for them to write their responses. "I put the green box next to the red box." He puts the green box back in the red box. He continues this process 5 to 10 times.

■ Later, students can be expected to say or write out the actions. For instance, Mr. George asks the students to identify what he is doing with the red box to solicit such responses as "opening it," "closing it," or "putting it on the table." This could be practice or review of present tense participles—in which the students learn to use "-ing" verb endings.

Example 5: Adaptation to Content—SEI 2 and 3 and Mainstream

Not only can this process be extended into the teaching of grammatical elements such as verbs, prepositions, or adjectives, but also into various content areas in the mainstream classes where LEP children have been placed. For instance, students can be directed to manipulate blocks, learn geometric shapes, or put magnets into places on a globe to learn geography. It should move from the simple to the complex.

MOVING FORWARD: MINIMAL VERBAL RESPONSES

Example 1: One-Word Replies—SEI 1

Within a few days or weeks, depending on individual differences and the students' overall exposure to English, students will come to the point where they are willing and able to respond verbally in the SEI 1 classroom. They will be provided opportunities to speak freely, as is explained in later chapters. However, during the class time devoted to building listening skills, verbal responses should be kept minimal. This allows the students to focus on what they are hearing without worrying about constructing entire phrases as responses.

Visual aids enhance these activities and can be ordered through publishing companies that are listed at the end of this chapter.

■ *Colors.* Mrs. Dahl uses visuals in teaching the students to identify three or four colors. As she displays the appropriate picture, she directs, "This is the color red. Say 'red.'" "What color is it again?" "This is blue. Say 'blue.'" "What color is this?" "Tell me the color as I point to each picture." After the students have mastered the naming of the colors, she can proceed to a variation of TPR.

■ *Colors and common objects.* Mrs. Dahl points to objects in the classroom and asks, "What color is this book? This pencil? Maria's dress? Daniel's shoes? My earrings?" She holds up a picture and puts her finger on details, one at a time: "The sky is . . . The flowers are . . . The grass is . . ." As she works with the students on colors, she is giving them the opportunity to learn to become familiar with the names of various objects as well.

■ *Fewer cues.* Mrs. Dahl stays focused on particular objects and uses the same vocabulary until the students can identify the colors without her having to point to the particular objects. "What is the color of the sky in this picture? Is the grass red? What color is the grass?" At the end of this 15-minute lesson, the students will not only have practiced the naming of colors, but also will have increased their listening vocabularies by as many as 25 words.

■ *Put it all together.* Mrs. Dahl brings in words that have already been learned. "Does Omar have white shoes on?" "In what objects around the room do we see the color red?" The teacher encourages movements and one-word responses from the students, "Oscar, go to the table below the window in front of the class. Pick up the picture of a man standing in front of a house and show it to the class. Point to the man's face. What color are his eyes?"

Example 2: More With Visuals—SEI 1

After the students have learned numbers, colors, and basic descriptive words, Mrs. Dahl continues to build on the students' listening comprehension through visuals. She tells a story with pictures of the main characters and objects. If she does not have the right visuals, she draws the figures on the blackboard. Also, usually from Grade 4 up, there are artistic students who are glad to create the visuals for her; of course, she can turn to the art teacher for assistance in this area. She stays on one picture at a time until the students show mastery. She then proceeds to the remaining pictures.

■ *Picture 1.* Mrs. Dahl speaks as she holds up a picture of a tall, thin man. "This is Mr. Jones. He is tall and thin, has dark brown hair, is about 35 years old, and is wearing a blue suit." Mrs. Dahl checks for vocabulary by asking, "What is the opposite of tall? What color is the suit?" Then she asks the entire class, "Is the man's name Mr. Jones?" "Is Mr. Jones short?" The students answer, "Yes!" and then "No!" Mrs. Dahl continues this, asking for only yes/no replies. First she asks the questions to the entire group, then to individual students.

■ *Compare Pictures 1 and 2.* Mrs. Dahl shows the next picture, which is of Mrs. Jones, who is short, about 30 years old, and married to Mr. Jones. Then Mrs. Dahl puts the two pictures next to each other on the board. She explains, "Tell me whom I am talking about, Mr. Jones or Mrs. Jones." She proceeds as follows:

"Who is the man?" "Who is the woman?"

"Who is tall?" "Who is short?"

"Who is 35 years old?" "Who is 30 years old?"

"Who is married to Mrs. Smith?"

"Who has dark hair?" "Who has blonde hair?"

"Who is wearing a suit?" "Who is wearing a dress?"

Mrs. Dahl mixes up the questions to make sure that the students are truly understanding. This continues until Mrs. Dahl is satisfied that each student has grasped the vocabulary.

■ *Compare Pictures 1, 2, and 3.* Next, Mrs. Dahl puts up a third picture of John, the son of Mr. and Mrs. Jones. She describes the child and goes through the same process as she did with the pictures of John's parents. She puts the three pictures on the board and asks similar questions, but now they include questions about the boy. She adds a picture of John's sister. The process continues. She also might include pictures of pets and the house that the family lives in.

TPR as Format for All SEI Levels and the Mainstream

Offering students the chance to listen to the simplest of descriptions that build into the complex can be used in all areas of instruction. The principles of TPR can be used for teaching stories and even the more complex material that has to do with content.

Example 1: From Details to Complete Story

As soon as the students can comprehend the vocabulary for three to five pictures, Mrs. Dahl tells a story using those pictures and points to the appropriate picture as she speaks. She stops occasionally to ask questions that call for the names of the characters, such as, "Who was the last to leave the table?" or yes/no responses, such as, "Is Maria still sad?" The entire process takes about 30 minutes.

Example 2: Compare Pictures

This format increases in difficulty with the students' growing ability to understand what they hear and their advancement into the higher levels of SEI. The teacher can pick up a variety of posters at any school supply store and use them for students to make comparisons. For instance, five numbered pictures of American landscapes can be carefully explained one at a time and then set against the chalkboard. The teacher asks, "In what picture do you see the skyscrapers of a large city?" Students respond, "Three!" The teacher proceeds, "In what picture is there a farm with a house, a barn, and a field?" Students respond, "Five!" The teacher continues the process of soliciting number responses from the entire class or group, and then calls on individual students. Gradually, the teacher can move into asking for more specific information: "How many buildings in the third picture appear to be more than 10 stories high?" or "Look at the fifth picture. About how many feet is the farmhouse from the barn?"

Incorporate Into the Content Area. The students can respond in a like fashion to the teacher's questions about pictures of the universe, historical events, food types, and so on. "Look at the picture of the universe and count the planets that revolve around the sun." "Go to the map and point to the states that fought with the Union in the Civil War." "Here are several cans of foods; choose one and then put it into the box that identifies its food group."

Example 3: Story Telling—All SEI Levels and Mainstream

From the early stages of SEI classes, the teacher can read various pieces of literature to the students or present them by means of CD-ROMs, cassettes, or videos. The teacher begins by introducing the story in an interesting way and explaining the new vocabulary by means of visuals. In the first 4 to 6 weeks of SEI instruction, the stories should be offered in small segments that last no more than a minute or two. The time should be increased gradually to 5 and then 10 minutes. The teacher paces these listening sessions to what the students can handle easily.

It is helpful to check the students' comprehension immediately. This can be done quickly by having the students write down whether four or five statements are true or false:

"When King Arthur was a boy, he lived with his father."

"Sir Lancelot fell in love with Guinevere."

"Guinevere married Sir Lancelot."

"Sir Lancelot's castle was called Camelot."

The teacher will soon know if the students have understood what they heard. It may be necessary to read the story again or replay the CD-ROM, cassette, or video. Students can be given a list of detail questions to answer as they listen to a story for a second or third time.

Example 4: Build Vocabulary Through TPR Variation—SEI Levels 2 and 3 and Mainstream

For those literate students in SEI classes or even in the mainstream, 10 to 30 words can be put on the board and then introduced or reviewed. After going over the definitions of the vocabulary that the students may or may not have had before, the teacher asks the students to choose among the words on the board in response to his or her questions:

"When we are talking about the distance around an object, which word do we use?"

"I want to study something that is extremely small, much too tiny to see. I must use a . . ."

"If a person is visiting a foreign country and his passport is lost or stolen, the person should go to the . . ."

The hints should be worded differently from the definitions because the point is to help the students internalize those words, not to memorize their meanings. It helps immensely for the words to be on the board because, for

English language learners, it is difficult to recall the words without that extra help of visualization. This technique does not hinder the learning of the native speakers in a mainstream class; they will appreciate the opportunity to review important vocabulary in a simplified format.

IMPROVING LISTENING SKILLS THROUGH READING AND WRITING

As students learn to read English at any level of English proficiency, they can follow the script of a story or lesson while listening to a cassette recording of that script that has been purchased or made beforehand by the teacher, the aide, or another student.

- After the first reading, students identify and find out the meanings of the words they do not know, either independently or with guidance from the teacher.
- The students listen to the story or lesson a second or third time while reading the script. They review the new words.
- The students listen to the story or lesson for a third or fourth time without the script.
- Finally, after the students have become confident that they know the story or lesson, they receive a copy of a new script with many words missing. They listen closely and fill in the missing words.
- An alternate activity would be for the students to divide into pairs or groups to list the most important information about the story or lesson.
- Other possibilities would be for the students to write questions about the story or lesson, or to turn the story or lesson into a dramatization to be recorded and played back.

Students benefit from additional activities that combine listening with writing, such as dictations and the retelling of information using specific vocabulary. Anything that provides these students the opportunity to listen repeatedly to important information and then to respond in some way can help them improve their understanding of English while mastering the subject matter. This will be discussed at length in the next chapters.

CAUTIONS: NOT EVERYONE UNDERSTANDS AT THE SAME RATE

1. The ability to discriminate sounds varies from student to student. This becomes evident very early in a structured English immersion SEI Level 1 class of students who started out knowing no English. Some students will understand the language rapidly and soon be ready to move on to the next lesson, whereas others will require a lot more practice. All these children should receive what they need, whether it's more challenge, more practice, or simply more of the same type of instruction.

2. The teacher must have flexible options. Some activities can be taught to the whole class whereas others must be accomplished in groups. It makes sense to offer those children who can quickly understand the language the opportunities to move at a faster pace. Students who are struggling should be provided with more opportunities to practice. Lessons can be speeded up, slowed down, and kept on course with the help of a teacher's aide, a peer tutor from another class, a tape recorder, and/or a computer.

3. The youngsters who need more challenge can read or listen to stories by means of headsets connected to tape recorders or computers. In keeping with TPR principles, it works best if the students have to respond with movements as they listen to these stories. This works with a computer because, as the students view choices on the screen, they can respond with their fingers on the mouse or the keyboard.

4. There should always be a time in the day for children to receive reinforcement in areas where they have difficulty. An aide or peer tutor can play "Simon Says," Picture or Word Bingo, or a similar game with the children who need more practice on specific vocabulary. There should be chants and songs available as well to help with this process.

5. All this takes planning and organization. Because some students will move quickly through the levels, it is advisable for all of the SEI classes to be scheduled at the same time, or at least to be aligned in ways that make transition from one level to the next as smooth as possible. Possibly, the SEI teachers can share some activities so that the students become acquainted with teachers outside of their main classroom. This way the students won't become apprehensive when they have to move on to another teacher.

6. Some schools have a large enough LEP population that three levels of SEI can be established in three different class-rooms. In this case, the teachers need to collaborate and share experiences frequently with each other. It is important for the teachers to trust that the other teachers will do a good job with the students whom they are moving on.

CHECKLIST AND REMINDERS

The following principles should be followed in teaching lis-tening skills to English language learners of any age:

- Some students need to listen to something more times than others. Aides, peer tutors, cassette players, and computer programs should be set up to allow for this to happen.
- Students should not be required to speak before they are ready.
- Students will remember best if they respond physically to the language. This can be done through body or even

hand movements such as drawing a picture, making a pencil mark, or clicking a computer key.

■ The students should advance from action responses to one-word verbal responses.

■ Sometimes it is necessary to slow down and simplify the language considerably in order for students to understand it.

■ Slang should be avoided in the early stages. It can be taught later on.

■ Visuals can be used very effectively to create memory pictures.

■ Like all skills, lessons are learned most easily if presented in a step-by-step format.

■ The language the students hear should be kept clear and authentic. When it is necessary for the language to be slowed down, it should flow naturally again as soon as possible.

■ Time should not be wasted on repeated attempts to explain an isolated word or phrase to a child in English. If someone in the room knows the word in that child's native language, that person should be called upon to explain it in the native language and then the lesson should resume immediately in English.

■ Structured English immersion is designed to use English as much as possible, so that almost any LEP student in Grades K–8 can be moved through the stages of immersion and into mainstream classes in 6 to 18 months at the most.

■ For high school students, separate SEI classes that encompass 1 to 3 class periods a day may be necessary for 2 to 3 years. This depends on the age of the students and the complexity of the material that they are expected to learn. The curriculum for those classes should be based on the mainstream curriculum as much as possible.

SELECTED RESOURCES FOR TEACHERS

Audiovisual Materials That Tell Stories or Present Broadcasts

- *Listen to Me!* by Barbara Foley, published by Heinle & Heinle (1-800-354-9706 or www.heinle.com), is a cassette/ workbook series that is quite excellent for all SEI levels of junior high and high school students. These very entertaining stories take about a minute to listen to and are accompanied by various listening exercises.
- *Los Andes Publishing Company* (1-800-532-8872 or www. losandeseducation.com) has available an ESL reading series with cassettes that include many American favorites such as *King Arthur and His Knights, Pocahontas, Zorro, Robin Hood,* and the like. These stories are appropriate for English language learners from Grades K–8.
- *Steck-Vaughn* (1-800-531-5051 or www.steck-vaugh. com) offers award-winning class sets of fiction and nonfiction books, which include CD-ROMs, created distinctly for the various levels of second language learners in the early grades.
- *Tapestry Listening & Speaking,* also by Heinle & Heinle, is a video/workbook series for older children that is based on authentic CNN news broadcasts, interviews, conversations, and debates.

Audiovisual supplementary support for content-area classes

- *Connections* by Steck-Vaughn is a CD-ROM series for Grades 5 through 8 that provides assistance in mathematics, science, and/or social studies.
- *Skillbuilders* by Heinle & Heinle is a workbook/cassette program that is based on standards in language arts, science, math, and social studies for Grades 5 through 12.

Pictures and Posters

- *SRA Photo Library* by SRA/McGraw-Hill (1-800-201-7103 ext. 6 or www.sra4kids.com) includes 210 pictures in each of three sets that cover 15 categories.
- *60 Wall Charts* available from Oxford University Press (1-800-451-7556 or www.oup-usa.org/esl/) feature poster-size reproductions of various topics.

3

Incorporating Content Area Curriculum Into Instruction

Within a month or two of being immersed in English, most structured English immersion (SEI) students can make fairly accurate approximations of their teachers' English and begin preparation to enter regular classes. This is the result of their having accustomed themselves to their teachers' facial expressions, gestures, and frequently used vocabulary. Total Physical Response (TPR) exercises have given SEI students the listening practice that makes it automatic for them to focus on key words in order to make sense of context. For instance, a third-grade teacher may give the following directions to a class that is either made up of SEI students exclusively or includes both SEI students and native English speakers:

> Boys and girls, take out your books. Turn to page 26, where we will read a story about a boy who lost his dog. The boy was very sad because he loved his dog very much. Maybe some of you have had a dog and understand

how the boy felt. Let's go into our groups to read the story. Stand up and take your chair to the group you belong to. I will walk around and listen to you read aloud.

The SEI students may have understood no more than 30% of what they heard:

Boys and girls, books . . . page . . . read story . . . boy lost dog . . . boy sad . . . go groups . . . read story . . . Stand up and take chair . . . I walk . . . you read.

SEI students often respond with the appropriate actions despite the fact that they have comprehended only a fraction of what was said. Better understanding is likely if the teacher writes numbers and key words on the board or shows pictures while speaking. It also helps if the schedule of the various classroom activities follows a regular routine, so the students can count on a certain amount of predictability. Meanwhile, it is important to realize that at this stage the students have developed listening and survival skills, not fluency.

LEARNING TO SPEAK ENGLISH TAKES TIME

Expressing a new language is much more difficult than interpreting it; thus, the students' speaking ability will develop more slowly than their listening comprehension. How long it takes for a child to speak with fluency that approaches that of a native speaker depends on many factors such as the child's age, how different the first language is from English, the child's ability to adapt to change, and the child's learning habits.

CORRECTNESS MATTERS

As students begin to speak English, it is normal for them to insert the vocabulary of the new language into the syntax of the native language. For example, "No tengo dinero" in Spanish becomes "No have money" in English, which can be easily understood, although not considered acceptable English. This type of speech pattern is commonly referred to as "interlanguage" and is considered a step in the process of becoming proficient in English. For this reason, at the early stages, fluency takes precedence over correctness. However, correctness should not be ignored. As students practice and master grammatical structures, it is important to gently encourage them to incorporate what they have learned into their speech and writing.

Example 1: "S" Ending of Present Tense Verb

The student says, "My brother work at the factory." SEI 1 teacher Mrs. Dahl remarks to the student new to English, "Your brother works (with emphasis on the "s") at the factory. Right?" The student nods. If the student is in the process of learning about the "s" ending, Mrs. Dahl reminds the student about the rule by asking, "What does (emphasis on the "s") your brother do?" The student replies, "works at the factory." If Mrs. Dahl has taught the rule to mastery, but the student has relapsed, Mrs. Dahl holds up her index finger to remind the student that he or she is talking about one person (third person, singular subject). The student will likely say, "Oh yeah, I forgot. My brother works at the factory."

Example 2: "Don't"

Something as difficult as "don't" can be handled in a similar fashion. The student tells Mr. George, the SEI 2 teacher, "No have book." If the student hasn't learned the correct structure, Mr. George models it: "You don't have a book, Right?" The student nods. If the student has learned "don't" as a construction, Mr. George says, "What don't you have?" The student continues, "I don't have a book." "Right! I will get you one," replies Mr. George with a smile.

SETTING UP ACADEMIC GOALS

It is essential to set up specific benchmarks for SEI students to meet at each juncture along the way. These goals must be arranged so students have the opportunity to practice elements of English syntax while learning the vocabulary of the designated lessons and background material that the mainstream teachers deem most important.

In some schools, each grade is required to align its subject matter with district and state curriculum standards. In other schools, the curriculum standards are not well defined. In the former, the planning for SEI classes can be done fairly easily; in the latter, it will take more effort and collaboration with mainstream teachers. However in either case, certain points become evident.

Some English structural patterns are taught to both native speakers and new English learners but with different emphasis. Children in the early grades who have grown up in an environment where Standard American English (SAE) has been the dominant language are likely to speak the language with reasonable correctness automatically whereas new English learners will grope for words simply to convey their message as quickly as possible. Native speakers of SAE are not likely to say, "I comes to school yesterday," because they have mastered the correct language structures unconsciously. For them to learn subject/verb agreement or verb tense is a clarification of something already familiar to them. They can trust that a particular language structure is correct most of the time because "it sounds right."

New English learners cannot rely on their intuition to speak English correctly because they will inadvertently use the patterns of their native language unless taught otherwise. For them, the process is slower and requires a lot more practice. Nevertheless, both groups should be able to demonstrate mastery of basic grammatical structures such as subject/verb agreement and verb tense by the end of the third grade, according to the language arts standards of many states' departments of education.

What is automatic to native speakers has to be taught to new English learners. Like all languages, English has its own characteristics. This includes word order, verb tense, construction of questions, formation of clauses, pronunciation, inflection, and intonation. The younger the child, the more likely it will be for him or her to acquire some of these linguistic elements informally through exposure to the language. However, more often than not, children will profit from lessons aimed at helping them over predictably difficult linguistic hurdles.

New English learners are able to learn the same subject matter as the native speakers. Content-area material for SEI classes should be aligned as much as possible with that of the mainstream curricula in preparing these students for their transition into the mainstream. To accomplish this, the SEI teachers must consult with the mainstream teachers to develop a reasonable plan. A certain amount of simplification and condensation will be necessary. Also, the SEI students can be taught how to grasp the main points of text written above their language ability.

CREATING THE CURRICULA

SEI classes are divided into three sections, each having its own separate curriculum. SEI 1 introduces students to the basic vocabulary and grammar necessary to function in an English-speaking environment. The students develop listening skills and practice simple oral exercises while learning fundamental literacy skills that are aligned with some basic skills learned in the early primary grades. SEI 2, composed of second and third graders, and SEI 3, usually composed of children in Grade 4 and above, offer students opportunities to continue to improve listening skills and to generate their own speech with more complex sentence structures. At SEI 2 and 3, the students improve reading and writing skills through lessons developed from the mainstream curricula.

In creating curriculum for each level, SEI teachers take the following steps:

1. They pull information from the mainstream curriculum guides and textbooks.

2. They consult with the mainstream teachers.

3. They construct their own curriculum guides—often as a school or district team.

Pulling Information From Mainstream Sources

While reading through what the mainstream teachers plan to cover in a particular subject area, the SEI teachers prioritize what is most important and feasible for their students. They look through curriculum guides that are typically divided into subgroups that make it possible to separate the main points from the segments. They examine the corresponding textbooks, paying close attention to chapter summaries and reviews. Both sources contain material from which lessons for SEI students can be created. Whatever is covered in both the curriculum guide and textbook is probably most important. Separating the essential from the not so essential is the first step in creating curricula for the SEI classes.

Collaboration With Mainstream Teachers

The SEI teachers take the condensed curricula to the subject matter teachers to be sure they've included what is necessary background information for entry into the mainstream classrooms. These teachers work together as a team to make sure the curricula are kept as condensed and specific as possible. The goal must be that the students learn the most important information thoroughly. This plan is always subject to revision; supplementary lessons can be included for fast-moving students and/or whatever time remains after the basic lessons have been completed.

Ideally, the sequence of presentation should coincide with that of the mainstream so students can attend those classes at any time and have a general idea of what is going on. However, the students' mastery of the information at hand should always be given higher priority than keeping to any schedule.

Pronunciation, Intonation, and Inflection

The SEI teacher listens closely to the students to catch the faulty sounds or patterns, repeats words using the correct sound or pattern two or three times, and then lets the student(s) practice. However children are never put on the spot in front of the entire class or browbeaten into correct pronunciation. The teacher makes it a rule that students are not allowed to laugh at each other's mistakes. When a child says a seemingly difficult-to-pronounce word correctly, the teacher praises that student.

For a small amount of time, possibly 10 minutes in the morning, students can practice pronunciation, intonation, and inflection. The SEI teacher exaggerates the sentence patterns, such as "I DO like cake, Don't you?" (The voice rises and extends upward in pitch with "you.") Students repeat several similar constructions after the teacher.

The inflection at the end of a question is easy for most new English learners to imitate, but it sounds so strange to them that they feel foolish doing so. They can practice this as a group. Also, the students and teacher can clap the rhythms of simple sentences as though they were chants.

See the resource section at the end of this chapter for books of chants that have been created for LEP students.

Reading

LEP students will vary greatly in their ability to read according to age, prior experience, and native language. Whereas it is the nature of any class of English language learners to practice comprehension skills through listening and speaking, often the basic decoding problems are overlooked due to the urgency in developing auditory/oral skills. Some students who are literate in their first language develop literacy in English quickly and easily. However, other LEP students may comprehend what they hear reasonably well but have difficulty with the written page because they have not learned to read in their native language or their decoding skills have not transferred adequately from their native language to English. Whereas those students who can decode words easily should move ahead into the comprehension skills that are an important part of all content areas, the children who cannot decode words adequately must receive the help they need.

The research indicates that literacy problems can be avoided from the beginning for "at-risk" children by offering them "systematic, explicit, and intensive instruction in phonemic awareness, phonics, reading fluency, vocabulary, and reading comprehension strategies," according to the statement presented in 2001 to a U.S. House of Representative subcommittee on education by Dr. G. Reid Lyon, Chief of the Child Development and Behavior Branch of the National Institute of Child Health and Human Development (NICHD). His conclusion was based on studies completed by the NICHD, the Office of Education Research and Improvement (OERI), the Office of Special Education Programs (OSEP), and the National Science Foundation (NSF).

Some effective, systematic phonics programs that have proven invaluable in teaching all children the aforementioned literacy skills are listed at the end of this chapter. Teachers can teach the lessons to the new English learners exactly as these programs suggest that they be taught to mainstream students, but generally more time should be allotted for completion of the exercises. These programs provide frequent short tests to indicate when the students are ready to move on.

Reading instruction should be scheduled in such a way that all children in the school have reading at the same specific time. This makes it possible for many LEP students to be mixed with mainstream students as they make progress. Both LEP and mainstream students can learn in small groups that focus on particular skills and then advance into other groups as they improve.

Beyond the specific reading program(s), the SEI teachers can provide general help in decoding and comprehension skills as part of various content-area reading activities.

Writing

Writing is not emphasized at SEI 1, but can be incorporated into lessons. On the other hand, SEI 2 and 3 students write every day—both freely and with the purpose of improving their style. They maintain journals and prepare short paragraphs, much like the mainstream students.

The teacher may duplicate a particularly outstanding student work so that other students can discuss and use it as a model, as long as the student writer has given his or her permission. Also, the SEI 2 and 3 students can improve their writing by correcting other students' errors.

Example: Sentence Revising

Ms. Garcia, an SEI Level 3 teacher, pulls a sentence from an unidentified student's writing and puts it on the board: "my brother not come to school because was sick." She asks the students to rewrite the sentence with the three corrections that it needs. The students complete the exercise on small pieces of paper in a couple of minutes, hand them to the teacher, and then write in their journals. During the journal writing, Ms. Garcia quickly goes through the small pieces of paper and gives "bonus" credits to the students for each correct change to the sentence. After the journals have been collected, the teacher passes back the corrected pieces of paper to the students. Writing on the board, she goes through the proper changes, one by one, with the students. About 3 days later, Ms. Garcia writes a similar sentence on the board: "I do not eat lemons because are sour." This sentence contains the same error that most students did not identify in the original sentence. With a second chance, most students can now make the proper correction. If some students still cannot identify the error, she knows to take them aside and work with them individually.

Social Studies as a Tool for Improving Literacy

The social studies books may appear overwhelming to the SEI 2 and 3 students. Taken in small doses, the social studies material is within the students' scope of comprehension. The following steps can be followed either in their entirety or in parts. Virtually everything in the social studies section can be applied to other subject areas as part of literacy development.

Example 1: Introduction

Ms. Garcia has carefully picked a lesson that will be both interesting and necessary to the students. She offers a short introduction, such as, "Today we are going to learn about a very famous man in U.S. history, Thomas Jefferson. Does anyone know anything about him?" She mentions when Jefferson lived and some of his accomplishments, followed by about five new vocabulary words that she puts on the board and then explains.

Example 2: Overview

Ms. Garcia reads a few paragraphs of the text aloud at a moderate pace to the students. She stops occasionally to ask questions that can be answered from the text and explains what they may not understand: "Where did Jefferson live when he became inaugurated as president?" (Response: "In a boarding house in Washington, D.C.") "Do you know what a boarding house is?" (Various responses and then an explanation from the teacher.)

Example 3: Echo Reading

Ms. Garcia invites the students to read aloud after her. She slows down her speed slightly and stops for a second or two at each period. Initially Ms. Garcia's voice is the loudest, but as the students improve their reading pace, Ms. Garcia's voice fades into the background.

Example 4: Constructing Questions

Ms. Garcia requests the students to construct a few questions that the text answers. She puts the students' questions on the board. She brings up a few more details and has the students construct more questions from that information.

Example 5: Reciprocal Reading

Ms. Garcia arranges the students in pairs. She instructs them to read aloud to each other. They cover the same material that Ms. Garcia has read to them. Student A reads a paragraph aloud to Student B. Student A asks Student B two or three questions about that paragraph. Student B answers those questions and then reads aloud the next paragraph to Student A. This is followed by Student B's questioning of Student A. If a student misses a question, the other student tells him or her the answer. The students take turns until the assigned reading is completed. During this time, Ms. Garcia walks around to help students with text that still confuses them.

Example 6: Summarizing

Ms. Garcia draws from the students' five statements that are most important to the story, such as these: "Thomas Jefferson became inaugurated as third president." "He wanted a government that did not interfere with people's lives." "He owned a big house in Virginia and had about 200 slaves." "His government spent 15 million dollars on the Louisiana Purchase." "The Louisiana Purchase doubled the size of the United States." The students discuss these statements.

Example 7: Dictation

Ms. Garcia helps the students to read and learn to spell words such as *Louisiana, Jefferson, government,* and *inaugurated* by having the students sound out the word backwards as she adds letters, usually from left to right:

na	on	men	ted
ana	son	ment	rated
siana	erson	ernment	gurated
isiana	efferson	vernment	augurated
Louisiana	Jefferson	government	inaugurated

After practicing the difficult words, the students write out the five sentences twice. They dictate the sentences back and forth to each other. After being allowed time to study the sentences either in the classroom or as homework, Ms. Garcia dictates the sentences to the students as a quiz. Every spelling and punctuation error is circled by the teacher and then handed back to the students for them to rewrite correctly.

Recent research indicates that dictation exercises improve students' use of grammatical structures by enabling them to focus on the particulars of sentence structure and spelling (Morris & Tremblay, 2002, pp. 364-385).

Example 8: Deciphering Complex Sentences

When students have difficulty with an unusually long sentence, Ms. Garcia shows them how to analyze it through skills learned in SEI 1, as follows:

On July 4, 1826, the 50th anniversary of the Declaration of Independence, both Adams and Jefferson lay dying.

Teacher	Student Response
"What are the prepositional phrases?"	"On July 4, 1826," "of the Declaration," and "of Independence"
"Now let's find the main verb."	"lay dying"
"So who lay dying?"	"Adams and Jefferson"
"Put the subject and main verb together."	"Adams and Jefferson lay dying"

"What is celebrated on July 4, 1826?"	"The anniversary of the Declaration of Independence"
"So what is most important?"	"Adams and Jefferson died on the same day."
"What day was that?"	"July 4, 1826"

Without such an exercise, LEP children can easily misunderstand the sentence so much that they believe it to be about the Declaration of Independence rather than the two men.

Example 9: Retelling

Ms. Garcia puts approximately eight words and phrases from the story on the board to be used as prompts: "Thomas Jefferson," "in Virginia," "200 slaves," "inaugurated," "third president," "a government that did not interfere," "Louisiana Purchase," and "doubled." Ms. Garcia leads the students through the process of retelling the story with the prompts and puts what they say on the board. It results in something similar to the following:

> Thomas Jefferson lived in Virginia. He had 200 slaves. He was inaugurated and became third president of the United States. He did not want a government that interfered with the people's lives. His government paid for the Louisiana Purchase. That doubled the size of the United States.

After study in class or as a homework assignment, the students prepare to retell the story as another quiz. They may put the paragraph in their own words, but must use the eight words and phrases that are provided for them on the board or in handouts as prompts. The students are graded for spelling, punctuation, usage, and using the eight words and phrases.

Example 10: Journal Writing

SEI 2 and 3 students write at least four sentences in a journal daily. The teacher reads every journal entry for its content and writes a short response. The subject can include a word that the students had difficulty with, a review question, or something else that is relevant to the class. The teacher writes the words that start the journal entry for the day. It could be, "If I were inaugurated as president of the United States, I would . . . ," "Thomas Jefferson . . . ," "I like (do not like) Thomas Jefferson because . . . " With journal writing, the students have the opportunity to write freely and communicate privately with their teacher. From this back-and-forth communication, the relationship between each student and the teacher grows. Also, the teacher can identify frequent error tendencies in grammar, usage, or punctuation from this daily writing. This can be addressed to the entire class as part of "sentence revising."

Example 11: Sentence Combining

Ms. Garcia writes on the board: "Thomas Jefferson was the third president. He lived in a big house in Virginia. He had about 200 slaves." Ms. Garcia works with the students to construct a new sentence and writes it on the board: "Thomas Jefferson, who was the third president, lived in a big house and had about 200 slaves." She shows students another construction: "Thomas Jefferson, the third president, lived in a big house and had about 200 slaves." After these examples, Ms. Garcia has the students work in threes or pairs to figure out more combinations.

Other activities can be developed to help students improve literacy while preparing for mainstream social studies. They can use their own questions to create contests similar to quiz shows on television. The students can review an important sentence through a "hangman" game format in which teams take turns naming letters until they can figure out how the entire sentence reads. They can be taught to outline information. They can put on skits in which they act out the parts of leaders.

Mathematics

It takes a great deal of daily effort for new English learners to develop automatic understanding of numbers in English. Some activities for this are as follows:

- The teacher points to numbers; the students identify them as a group and then individually.
- The teacher dictates numbers as students write them down at their desks or on the board.
- Students take turns saying numbers by ones, twos, and threes as a team contest.
- Students practice saying series of numbers both forward and backward.
- Students play "Number Bingo."

Place value is often very difficult for new English learners and should, therefore, be practiced.

Example: Place Value

Mr. George shows students the process by having them write numbers down as he reads them. After doing this, he immediately provides the correct answer:

Teacher	Students Write
Fifteen	15
One hundred fifteen	115
One thousand one hundred fifteen	1,115
Sixteen thousand one hundred fifteen	16,115

He practices several numbers in this way and then lets students compete in teams as he reads off the numbers in mixed order.

As students move into complex mathematical problem solving, language becomes an issue for students who cannot understand their teacher's explanations. Manipulatives can assist the process. SEI teachers can use pictures and blocks to demonstrate geometric shapes and percentages, but that may not be enough. Fortunately, many older elementary children have already learned the concepts in their native language and just need to transfer the information into English. For those who just cannot understand, it may be necessary to find someone, a fellow student or an instructional aide or other adult, to explain the concept(s) in the native language. Also, tapes and/or CDs that offer explanations in the native language(s) may be kept on hand.

A mathematics program that has proven especially successful for LEP children is *Saxon Math* by Hake Saxon. The children learn math through a gradual development of concepts and continual practice. Also, the textbooks and workbooks are available in Spanish for fourth grade and above. At the end of this chapter is information on how to order this program.

Science

Science, especially that which requires the reading of a science text, generally follows the teaching of reading and math. However, even SEI 1 students can move into selected mainstream science classes when those classes are hands-on. As a supplement to a science activity, the teacher can have the students create a list of what they have learned from a science lesson and then put the list into chronological order. Each student can draw a picture of one thing that he or she remembers and then explain the picture to the class.

For 2 and 3, the teacher can modify the social studies strategies to teach the science text.

LOOKING FORWARD TO TRANSITION INTO THE MAINSTREAM

It is likely that the LEP children will fear "the mainstream," that place where they must compete with the non-LEP children. For this reason, the SEI teacher must resist the occasional temptation to depict the regular class as a place where the children will fail unless they master a particular lesson. It is much better to offer the students encouragement in the form of praise by mentioning that what they have just learned will help them in the mainstream class and/or that it is something that many mainstream students have difficulty with.

It is important that the students have several opportunities to visit the mainstream classes in which they will be eventually placed. It is also essential that they be given opportunities to talk about those experiences. Whereas it is impossible to totally erase the fear of change in these children, it is important to alleviate their discomfort as much as possible through positive means.

SELECTED RESOURCES FOR TEACHERS

Chants

- *Jazz Chants, Jazz Chants for Children, Jazz Chant Fairy Tales, Small Talk, Mother Goose Jazz Chants,* and *Grammar Chants* by Carolyn Graham at Oxford University Press (1-800-451-7556 or www.oup-usa.org/esl/) offer opportunities for students to practice pronunciation, intonation patterns, question inflections, and even grammatical patterns through exercises that are both rhythmic and entertaining.

Mathematics

- *Saxon Math* at Saxon Publishers (1-800-284-7019 or www.saxonpub.com) provides step-by-step sequences and many exercises that lead to mastery of each mathematical concept.

Systematic Phonics

- *Language! A Literacy Intervention Curriculum* by Jane Fell Greene and published by Sopris West (Kris Olyejar at

1-877-547-7323 or training@language-usa.net) prepares students to return to conventional curricula by advancing from where they are to where they should be according to grade placement.

■ *The Spalding Method* at Spalding Education International (1-877-866-7451 or www.spalding.org) presents a total language arts, multisensory system that allows students to learn the phonetic base of the language through listening, seeing, speaking, writing, spelling, and reading.

■ *SRA McGraw-Hill* (1-888-SRA-4543 or www.sra4kids. com) offers several programs:

– *Corrective Reading* offers remedial help to students in Grades 4 through 12 who have difficulty reading accurately and fluently.

– *Open Court Intervention Program* offers remedial help to children who are still struggling with reading skills in Grades 2 through 6. It consists of strategies for teaching phonics as well as high-interest/low-readability material that covers grade-level topics.

– *Open Court Phonics* provides the phonics elements of Open Court Reading in a separate format.

– *Open Court Reading* consists of instruction in both explicit phonics and comprehension skills. It is designed so all students can begin to read by the end of the first half of first grade. It is available for Grades K–6.

– *Reading Mastery* is a direct instruction program with scripted lesson plans for teachers. Students learn explicit phonics and comprehension skills through short lessons and instant feedback.

4

Organizing Structured English Immersion With the Focus on Basic Vocabulary and Grammar

Chapter 3 summarized how to prepare structured English immersion (SEI) students for the mainstream. This chapter offers more detailed information on how to do this with a focus on the teaching of grammar and language as well as some recommendations for the placement of SEI students.

SEI 1

SEI 1 is the entry level for all students who understand and speak either very little or no English. They have been identified as non-English speakers (NES) by the SEI teachers. SEI 1 lasts from 3 to 4½ months, depending on whether the school is divided into quarters or semesters.

The SEI 1 should be taught separate from SEI 2 and 3, if at all possible. SEI 1 students attend mainstream classes such as PE, music, art, and possibly hands-on science classes with students of their own age group. Special arrangements must be made for kindergarten and first-grade students to be put with their native English-speaking, same-age counterparts frequently.

Moving From Listening to Speaking

As SEI 1 students learn to understand basic English conversation, they begin to create their own responses. This is accomplished through oral language exercises that allow students the opportunity to practice everyday vocabulary and grammatical patterns. The vocabulary covers the following general topics:

parts of body	days of week	school	animals and plants
articles of clothing	months of year	home	the alphabet
cardinal numbers	seasons	family	occupations
ordinal numbers	telling time	food	colors and shapes

Other topics can be added or substituted in accordance with the students' ages and interests.

Every week, SEI 1 students focus on particular topics. They learn the vocabulary of those topics through Total Physical Response (TPR) exercises and stories presented to them by their teacher. After they have mastered the words and phrases of some topics, the teacher can lead the students into putting together their own skits that require the use of the words. The skits may deal with school situations, introductions, ordering food at a restaurant, shopping, or some other everyday function.

Example: Creating Skits

The students have learned the vocabulary for "articles of clothing" throughout the week. Mrs. Dahl draws out these words from the students and writes them on the board. She asks the students questions about where they buy clothes, what they say to the clerk, where they try on the clothes, and so on. As the students give their responses, Mrs. Dahl creates a short dialog that she writes on the board. She has the students write it down as best they can. The children go into groups of three or four and practice their own dialogs that are modeled after the dialog on the board. The students turn them into skits. Finally, each group acts out the skit. Mrs. Dahl provides several articles of clothing as well as dress-up clothes such as hats, ties, and shirts—which contribute to the drama and enjoyment of the activity.

SEI 1 LINGUISTIC EXPECTATIONS

SEI 1 students learn the most important aspects of grammar that help them understand the way English sentences are put together. Generally, after a day or two of 30- to 45-minute lessons, the follow-up exercises can be divided into two or three 10- to 15-minute segments during the day. The grammar elements should follow this suggested sequence:

1. Prepositions and prepositional phrases
2. Present tense of verb "to be"/person and number
3. Adjectives
4. Present tense/subject–verb agreement
5. Past tense
6. Future tense

The number of prepositions and verbs to be learned depends on the grade level. The teacher may identify grammatical elements as "adjectives" or "tense" but should not expect the students to either define or use the grammatical terminology themselves. As the teacher talks about the grammar, the students will come to understand what is meant by each term.

Time must be taken to introduce the grammatical concepts that have to do with "person" (first, second, and third) and "number" (singular and plural). Grasping "third-person singular" is the first step to understanding subject–verb agreement, a grammatical structure that is fundamental to gaining mastery over English in both speech and writing. Initially, the students learn that a third-person singular subject requires that an "s" be added to the main present-tense verb such as in "My mother *cooks* dinner." Later on, students who know this basic structure can easily pick up how a verb form or entire clause can be a "third-person singular" subject that requires that same "s": "Cooking dinner for our family *brings* my mother pleasure." Or, "That my mother cooks dinner for our family *shows* how much she loves us."

Prepositions and Prepositional Phrases

Coordinates with the identification of parts of the body, clothing, objects in the classroom, days of the week, months of the year, and seasons. First 3 to 5 weeks.

Prepositions are difficult in that they do not translate easily from one language to the other. For instance, a new English learner may say that he or she writes "to the blackboard" rather than "on the blackboard" because in the native language the equivalent expression requires a preposition that usually translates into English as "to." Also, to new English learners, it may seem odd to say "on the blackboard" because that preposition generally designates a position on top of something.

Many prepositions can be learned only through frequent use because there is often no logical explanation for why one preposition is used instead of another. For this reason, the grammar segments of the first 3 to 5 weeks of SEI Level 1 should emphasize the mastery of as many prepositions as possible and be taught as extensions of other lessons.

Example 1: Prepositional Phrases as an Extension of TPR

While Mrs. Dahl takes the children through several TPR exercises, the children become familiar with phrases such as "on your feet," "above your head," "over your eyes," "to the door," "into the room," "toward the ceiling," "on the desk," and so on. She builds on this with objects and pictures until the students can answer the following questions:

Teacher	Student Response
"Where are you sitting?"	"At my desk"
"Where is the pencil?"	"On the table"
"Where did I put the piece of paper?"	"Next to the pencil"
"Where did Laura lay her book?"	"Under her chair"
"Where am I walking?"	"Toward the door."

Mrs. Dahl makes it clear to the students that they are using "prepositional phrases."

Example 2: Identifying Prepositions in Reading

The students have just completed the oral reading of a short story. Mrs. Dahl directs the students, "Let's go back over the story and see if we can find all of the prepositional phrases." The students raise their hands with their replies. There may be a couple of phrases that the students have missed. Mrs. Dahl gives hints: "When did the phone ring?" A student responds, "During dinner." At this point the teacher offers other examples of "during" and lets the children create their own phrases with the preposition that they were not able to identify initially.

Example 3: Contrasting the Meanings of Prepositions

Students can practice prepositional phrases as they learn the days of the week, months, and seasons. They can learn to differentiate "before" from "after" in response to questions such as "What month comes after March?" or "What day comes before Wednesday?" This leads to the more difficult "When does spring come?" (Responses: "after summer," "before winter," and "between summer and winter"). They should practice "before" and then "after" on separate days before combining the two, so they do not confuse them.

Games can be developed such as "Prepositional Phrase Bingo" or guessing where a student has put an object ("Is it under the table?" "Is it near the door?").

Present Tense of the Verb "to Be" and Person/Number

Coordinates with learning numbers and various occupations. 1 to 2 weeks.

After a month's time, many students have an understanding of the personal pronouns, but have not yet mastered which "to be" word should be used with each pronoun.

Example 1: First-Person Singular

The teacher says, "I am Mrs. Dahl. Who are you?" Then she asks one volunteer at a time to identify himself or herself beginning with, "I am ... " Questions from the teacher or helper continue: "Are you a girl or a boy?" "Where are you from?" Each student responds, "I am a girl," or "I am a boy." "I am from ... "

This is a good time to teach numbers. Students can then answer the question, "How old are you?" with "I am ... years old."

Example 2: First Person With Visuals

Several pictures can be used to identify people in obvious activities and jobs. These pictures can be passed out to the students with the idea that each student represents the picture. One student announces, "I am a fireman. I am 30 years old." Another states, "I am a baker. I am 25 years old." The practice continues until all of the students are comfortable with using "I am."

Other similar exercises for lessons are developed on separate days in which the students become familiar with first-person plural, second person, and third-person singular and plural of present tense "to be" verbs. The teacher clarifies person and number to the students as they progress through the verb structures.

Adjectives

Coordinates with learning ordinal numbers, shapes, colors, animals, and plants. 2 to 4 weeks.

Children can now talk about their family members, pets, and where they live through descriptive words, most of which can be referred to as "adjectives."

Example 1: Family Tree

Mrs. Dahl uses a large picture of a family tree. A name and age is scrolled beneath each family member. After teaching the most common terms used for family members, she asks questions such as "Who is John's grandfather?" (Response: "Henry") and "Who is Mary's daughter?" (Response: "Susie"). After the students reach mastery, she advances to "What is Mary's relationship to Paul?" (Response: "Paul's sister") and "What are Robert and Sara to their children?" (Response: "father and mother"). Finally, Mrs. Dahl asks the students to describe various members of the family. A student explains, "Henry is the grandfather to John, Susie, Paul, and Mary. He is 65 years old. He is Martha's husband."

Example 2: Comparatives and Superlatives

Students can learn comparatives and superlatives. "Who is taller, Mario or Omar?" "Who is the youngest person in the class?" More difficult: "Are you younger or older than your brother?" "Is Maria younger or older than Thomas?" "Is Gabrielle's birthday before or after Robert's birthday?" "Who is a faster runner, you or your sister?" Students respond with complete sentences: "I am younger." "Maria is older." Gabrielle's birthday is before Robert's." "My sister is the faster runner."

Example 3: Ordinal Numbers

With similar activities, students can learn ordinal numbers: "Who is first in line?" or "Who sits in the fifth desk of the second row?" More difficult: "Explain where Juan sits."

Example 4: Adjective's Position Before Noun

Students learn to put the adjective before the word modified: "Omar is a tall boy." "My mother is a smart woman." "My pet is a brown dog."

There are many other activities for learning adjectives. Objects such as dolls, stuffed animals, or school tools can be passed around and discussed. As teams, students can take turns listing descriptive words, orally or in writing. Students describe themselves, each other, the teacher, family members, pets, their homes, and/or their artwork. They identify descriptive words in a colorfully written story. They write simple paragraphs based on those descriptions.

Present Tense/Subject–Verb Agreement

Coordinates with learning what to call various foods and how to tell time. 2 to 4 weeks.

The students have now been immersed for about two months. If they have not learned to tell time, they can do that now. Through personal experiences, pictures, and skits, the students identify what is going on using present tense verb forms with an emphasis on third-person singular subjects.

Example: Identifying Subject/Verb

Mrs. Dahl begins by telling the students to listen carefully as she asks questions. She solicits short answers from individual students to such questions as "What do you eat for breakfast, Monica?" "How do you come to school every day, Thomas?" "Where do you study, Vanja?" "What do you do after school, Maria?" and "What time do you go to bed, Georg?" After 5 to 10 questions have been answered, she asks volunteers to remember their classmates' responses in complete sentences:

Teacher	Student Response
"What does Monica eat for breakfast?"	"She eats cereal for breakfast."
"How does Thomas come to school each day?"	"He takes the bus to school."
"Where does Vanja study?"	"Vanja studies in her room."
"What does Maria do after school?"	"Maria does her homework after school."
"What time does Georg go to bed at night?"	"He goes to bed at 9 o'clock."

Mrs. Dahl writes the students' responses on the board. When a student errs, she does not correct the student, but, rather, writes the correct form of what was said. The students copy down the sentences.

Mrs. Dahl now asks the students to identify the prepositional phrases in the first sentence as a review. When one student replies, "at 9 o'clock," and another student, "to bed," Mrs. Dahl draws a line under each prepositional phrase. She instructs the students to find the prepositional phrases in the remaining sentences and to draw lines under them.

Their efforts should bring the following results:

Monica eats cereal <u>for breakfast</u>.

Thomas takes the bus <u>to school</u>.

Vanya studies <u>in her room.</u>

Maria does her homework <u>after school.</u>

Georg goes <u>to bed at 9 o'clock.</u>

From the words that remain, Mrs. Dahl has the students pick out the subject of each sentence. She explains, "Whom or what are we talking about? That is the subject of the sentence." Next she asks them to identify what the subject does or describes. She explains, "That is the main verb." She asks the students to draw a circle around the subject and a box around the main verb of each sentence. See Figure 4.1 for examples of what students are asked to do.

Figure 4.1

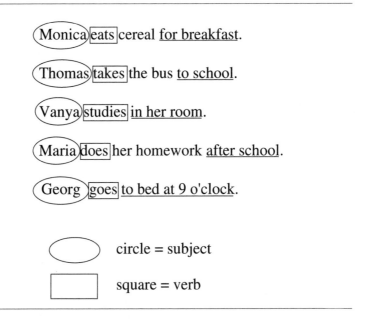

Mrs. Dahl calls attention to the "s" that is added to each main verb. She asks the students if they can figure out the reason for the "s." She reviews "person" as it was taught with the "to be" verbs and explains again that "third-person singular" subjects require "s" to be added to the main verb for present tense.

She raises her index finger frequently after that to remind the students when the subject is "third-person singular."

From that time forward, whenever the students run into a particularly complex sentence, Mrs. Dahl takes them through this process. The students draw lines under the prepositional phrases; after doing so, they can easily identify the subject and main verb.

Past Tense

Encompasses the vocabulary that has been learned to this point. 1 to 3 weeks.

The students are now able to understand commonly used past-tense verbs. Assimilating those verbs into their own speech is another matter.

Students from Asian countries such as Vietnam, Laos, or Thailand are used to languages where verb tense is nonexistent and time is established through other elements in the sentence. It is common for these students to ignore the entire concept of tense and to always use present-tense verb forms if not taught otherwise. This process must be explained step-by-step, especially for these children.

Example 1: Identifying Past Tense

Mrs. Dahl asks the students to list verbs and then she writes the present-tense forms on the board. Next, she asks for volunteers to give the past-tense form of each verb. She encourages them to draw on their prior knowledge: "What did the boy see? (Pause) The boy . . . " (Response: "The boy saw!") The teacher writes "saw" next to "see" and continues this process with the other verbs. She gives students the chance to use the past-tense verbs in simple sentences orally and in writing.

Example 2: Personalizing Past Tense

Mrs. Dahl puts time elements such as "yesterday," "this morning," "last week," and "two months ago" on the board or on large signs. A boy volunteers to talk about what he did while going through the motions of each action. "Yesterday I got up, took a shower, ate breakfast, and brushed my teeth." Another student says, "This morning I put on my clothes, combed my hair, and left the house." Following mastery, they can review present tense by following a similar format that is initiated by the phrase "Every day."

Example 3: Answering Questions in Past Tense

Question–answer segments can be spread throughout the day. The teacher asks the students questions that require them to use the past-tense form:

Teacher	Student
"What did you eat for dinner last night?"	"I ate stew."
"When did you go to bed?"	"I went to bed at 9 o'clock."
"How did you come to school?"	"I rode the bus."
"When did you do your homework?"	"I did my homework after school."
"What did you do at the park?"	"I played soccer."

The teacher can continue the exercise by asking the students the same questions that are now in the third person, such as "What did Lara eat for dinner?"

Such back-and-forth communication between teacher and student can be put into the other lessons. Also, while reading a story, students can transpose paragraphs either orally or in writing from present to past tense and vice versa. They can list past-tense activities such as "went to the movies" or "watched TV" as a team competition or play "past-tense" Bingo.

Future Tense

> *Review of all tenses and vocabulary learned to this point. 1 to 3 weeks.*

Students learn future tense through activities similar to those for the present and past tenses. They begin by acting out

"I will," "I shall," and "I am going to" sentences. They make plans for the next day or a future time and then review other tenses.

Example 1: Contrasting Verb Tenses

Once students are comfortable with the future tense, they should practice the three tenses together, possibly as a competition. One student talks about what he does every day: "I get up, I eat breakfast, I feed my dog, and I water the plants." Another student repeats the sentences in third person singular: "Every morning Paul gets up, he eats breakfast, he feeds the dog, and he waters the plants." A third student continues the sentences in past tense: "Yesterday Paul got up, he ate breakfast, he fed the dog, and he watered the plants." A fourth student puts the sentences into future tense: "On Wednesday Paul will get up, he will eat breakfast, he will feed the dog, and he will water the plants." A fifth student offers an alternative to the future: "Tomorrow Paul is going to get up, he is going to eat breakfast, he is going to feed the dog, and he is going to water the plants."

Example 2: Making Popcorn

Mrs. Dahl shows her students a popcorn popper, a bag of corn kernels, a bottle of vegetable oil, and some small paper bags. She identifies each object and then writes its name on the board. The students practice saying the words.

"What are we going to do today, class?" she asks the students. A student responds, "Make popcorn." "Right," the teacher replies as she looks around at all the students. "Everyone, what are we going to do? We are . . . " Students respond in unison, "We are going to make popcorn."

She continues drawing answers from the students: "What are we going to do first?" "What are we going to do after we heat the popper?" "What are we going to put into the popper?" "What are we going to do next?"

As Mrs. Dahl goes through the motions of preparing the popcorn, she calls on volunteers to verbalize what's going on. They respond with, "You put the kernels into the popper."

"We wait for the popcorn." "The popcorn smells good." "You put the popcorn into paper bags." "We are going to eat the popcorn."

After the popcorn has been prepared, Mrs. Dahl proceeds with the following:

Teacher	Student Response
"What did I do to make popcorn, Juan?"	"You put oil into the popper."
"What else did I do, Marco?"	"You put corn kernels into the popper."
"What did you hear from the popper, Ana?"	"I heard 'Pop!'"
"What did I put on the popcorn, Sara?"	"You put butter and salt on it."
"What are we going to do now, Hiro?"	"We are going to eat popcorn."

Mrs. Dahl asks students to come up with words to describe the popcorn. She puts those words on the board, discusses each one, and then has the students say them after her. She asks them questions that they can answer with the words on the board:

"How does it taste, Juan?"	"It tastes salty."
"How does it look, Henry?"	"It looks white."
"Touch it and tell me how it feels, Lara?"	"It feels soft."
"What does it feel like, Georg?"	"It feels like paper."

Simple exercises of grammar that allow students the opportunity to practice particularly difficult and relevant sentence structures make it possible for students to distinguish the syntax of English from that of their native language. Gradually, as fluency increases, these students incorporate what they have learned into their everyday speech and writing.

PLACEMENT AFTER SEI 1

Placement at the end of SEI 1 depends partially on the student's grade level. Ideally, the kindergarten and first-grade students will be ready to move into the corresponding mainstream classes at the end of SEI 1. The students in Grades 2 and 3 will be able to advance into SEI 2; and students in Grade 4 or above to SEI 3.

Unfortunately, there are always those students who were absent for many lessons, enrolled in school late, and/or did not do as well as expected. For some of the kindergarten and first-grade students, it may be advisable to develop an individualized plan for them to divide their time between SEI 1 and the mainstream classes.

No student should be held back for single deficiencies such as not being able to pronounce a sound or name the days of the week. Some time should be allowed at the end of SEI 1 instruction to review particular topics that some students have missed. The other students can be rewarded at that time by being allowed to listen to popular stories on audiotapes or to play word games together. Some of them may be willing to help the other students catch up.

The teachers who have worked with the children decide the students' placement. The teachers may test all the students at once and then retest students individually who do not fall easily into one group or the other. Teachers may want to use observations as well as standardized testing. Adjustments can be made at any time if there is evidence that a student was not placed correctly.

To comply with federal and state laws, the criteria for moving the students from one level to another, or especially into the mainstream, must be clearly defined. Good documentation on each child provides evidence that can be used to justify decisions made by the teachers. Also, solid data can help the district evaluate whether a program is effective or should be changed.

SEI 2 AND 3

Limited English Proficient (LEP) students in Grades 2 and above who understand everyday English conversation but still have difficulty putting their own sentences together are ready for instruction in SEI 2 or 3. These students have either met the standard to move beyond SEI 1 or scored at the lowest levels of limited English speaker (LES) according to a commercially developed English language assessment such as the IDEA Proficiency Test (IPT) or the Language Assessment Scales (LAS). When there is a conflict between the teacher's assessment and that of the commercial test, the teacher's assessment should have greater weight. Each of the two levels lasts from a semester to one full school year, depending on when the students enter and how fast they progress.

SEI 2 is composed of students in Grades 2 and 3, and SEI 3, of students above Grade 3. Keeping SEI 2 in a classroom separate from SEI 3 is recommended but not always possible because of lack of space, insufficient number of students, or lack of funding. If one teacher has to address both levels of SEI, at least one instructional aide should be available to help. While the SEI teacher is working on a lesson with the SEI 2 students, the aide can engage the SEI 3 students in other activities.

SEI 2 and 3 emphasize the material of mainstream subjects such as social studies and science, as explained in Chapter 3. Through collaboration with the mainstream teachers and good planning, the SEI 2 and 3 students can learn the fundamentals of the content area while learning to write simply and correctly. At these levels, the SEI teachers plan activities that bring the SEI students together with the mainstream students of the same age. That may happen with lessons that are conducted by either the SEI or mainstream teacher.

SEI 2 AND 3 LINGUISTIC EXPECTATIONS

At this point, most of the typical students' difficulty has to do with verbs. This includes constructing questions, progressive- and perfect-tense verbs, and passive voice. The teacher leads the students through a progression of lessons, similar to how verb constructions were practiced in SEI 1 lessons. However, students now spend more time using the structures in their writing.

Constructing Questions

The construction of present and past tense questions with "do," "does," "did," "don't," "doesn't," and "didn't" is extremely difficult for new learners of English. The students need to receive guidance on this as soon as possible because constructing questions is an important aspect of learning SEI 2 and 3 content. The students can begin by practicing emphatic "do" and "don't."

Example 1: "Yes, I do . . . " and "No, I don't . . . "

Ms. Garcia explains, "We can use 'do' and 'don't' to let someone know that we REALLY mean something. For instance, someone asks me if I like my students. I say, "Yes, I DO like my students. Now I want you to say, 'Yes, I DO' or 'No, I DON'T' to everything I ask and then finish the sentence."

Teacher	Student Response
"Do you ride the bus to school?"	"Yes, I DO ride the bus to school."
"Do you stay after school every day?"	"No, I DON'T stay after school every day."
"Do you eat vegetables every day?"	"Yes, I DO eat vegetables every day."

At the end of 8 to 10 question–answers, the students create their own questions with "Do you" and "Don't you." This lesson is followed by similar formats on following days that cover "Does he?," "Doesn't he?," "He DOES.," and "He DOESn't."

At another time, students practice "Did you . . . ?" and "Didn't you . . . ?" questions and answers. Finally, students are able to construct questions with interrogatives such as these: "When do you get up in the morning?" "Where do you live?" "What country did you come from?" "When did John Adams live?" "How do plants grow?"

Forming questions with the other tenses is not difficult because they are formed similarly to statements but with a change of word order. For instance, the question to "He *was walking* down the street" is "Where *was* he *walking*?"

These constructions can be practiced in short segments each day when there is extra time such as when students have finished their work about 5 minutes before the bell is due to ring.

Example 2: Questions From Answers

Ms. Garcia's students have learned how to form questions in all the tenses, but are not always able to do it automatically. Shortly before the noon break, Ms. Garcia asks the students to figure out the questions to her answers. The students volunteer their answers:

Teacher	Student Response
"I am going to the movies."	"Where are you going?"
"Georg likes to play soccer."	"What does Georg like to do?"
"Yesterday Maria went home early."	"When did Maria go home early?"

They continue until the bell rings.

At the end of an SEI 3 social studies lesson, Ms. Garcia offers more practice:

"They moved the capital to Washington."	"Where did they move the capital?"
"Jefferson believed in equality for men."	"What did Jefferson believe in?"
"Jefferson and Hamilton disagreed a lot."	"Who disagreed a lot?"

Progressive and Perfect Tenses

Students learn these tenses similarly to how they learned the other tenses. Also, the students can write down examples of the tenses that they find in their books and construct their own questions and answers. Most students find the progressive tenses easier to master than the perfect and perfect progressive tenses. The teacher may want to introduce the principal parts of verbs, listed in any dictionary, and have the students learn the ones most commonly used. With that, the teacher can ease the students into enjoyable oral exercises.

Example 1: Perfect Tense: "I have never . . . "

Mr. George has practiced the principal parts of about 10 verbs with the students through repetition drills in which the students repeated after him combinations such as "I see a movie, I saw a movie, I have seen a movie." Mr. George then instructs the students through examples to form perfect-tense sentences orally in response to his questions.

Teacher	Student Response
"Did you ever see a purple horse?"	"No, I have never seen a purple horse."
"Did you ever ride a kangaroo?"	"No, I have never ridden a kangaroo."
"Did you ever speak Latin?"	"No, I have never spoken Latin."

Students enjoy creating their own question–answer format for this.

Example 2: Perfect Progressive: "I have been ___ing"

After writing examples on the board and practicing them with the entire class, Mr. George starts off a question–answer exercise: "I have been teaching the class today. What have you been doing, Marta?" Marta replies, "I have been reading," and turns to Hiro: "What have you been doing, Hiro?" Hiro replies, "I have been writing a story, and what have you been doing, Georg?" And the process continues.

Passive Voice

Many new English learners cannot distinguish sentences such as "They have helped their people" from "They have been helped by their people." Consequently, what is assumed to be a problem of comprehension is oftentimes one of not being able to distinguish active from passive voice. For that reason, SEI students need to practice voice.

Example: Make the Object the Subject

Ms. Garcia throws a ball to Sofia. She asks the class, "What did I just do?" A student responds that she threw the ball to Sofia. Ms. Garcia replies, "That's right. Now explain what happened to the ball. Make 'the ball' the subject of the sentence." Most likely, the students will not be able to answer "The ball was thrown" unless they have already learned passive voice. Ms. Garcia explains the construction and gives many examples. Eventually, over several days, she takes them through each of the eight tenses with passive voice separately. Finally, they practice all eight forms of the passive tense, orally as before, changing verbs from active to passive:

Teacher	Student Response
"He sees the girl at school."	"The girl is seen at school."
"He spoke Spanish."	"Spanish was spoken."
"He will tell a story."	"A story will be told."
"He is reading a book."	"A book is being read."
"He was talking to his friend."	"His friend was being talked to."
"She has sold her bicycle."	"Her bicycle has been sold."
"They had understood the lesson."	"The lesson had been understood."
"We will have mastered the passive voice."	"The passive voice will have been mastered."

As students learn the verb structures, they can create posters that list the verbs in a way that makes sense to them. One poster may show questions; another, verb sequence; and still another, transition from active to passive voice.

The purpose is not for the students to become able to use all these verb structures themselves, but for them not to be confused when they read them in literature. Practicing verb structures in a systematic and enjoyable way enables the new English learners to gain control over what had previously seemed incomprehensible.

PLACEMENT AFTER SEI 2 AND 3

At the beginning or the end of the school year, teachers choose placement for each student from at least three options:

- Repeat Levels 2 or 3 for an additional semester or quarter
- Move from Level 2 to Level 3
- Move into a transitional situation in which extra assistance is available either within the mainstream classroom or in a separate resource room

It is up to the teachers to decide the criteria for each option. They may decide on specific scores from the English oral proficiency commercial test results, create their own measures, or combine the two. Generally, teachers will not run into difficulty with federal and state law as far as moving students from one level of special assistance to another as long as their criteria are well-defined and there is ample documentation on each child.

As students move from the SEI classes into the mainstream, most of them are still classified as LEP. This means that they must continue to receive special assistance unless the parents of the children insist that it stop. How to ensure that students receive support that enables them to succeed in mainstream classes will be discussed in Chapter 5.

5

Successful
Transitions

*Preparing Mainstream Classes for Structured
English Immersion Students*

Instructing limited English proficient (LEP) students can be
very rewarding. As young LEP students move into the mainstream, teachers soon discover that these students are typically
polite, demonstrate a determination to learn, and maintain
good attendance. Also, many LEP students and their parents
express respect and appreciation for their teachers' efforts.

Since the early 1970s, LEP students have spent years segre-
gated from the mainstream students in either bilingual
and/or long-term English as a second language (ESL) classes.
The rationale for this separation has been that either the LEP
students would fail miserably in the mainstream or that teaching both groups together would cause the academic standards
of the non-LEP students to decline. Not only can such
extremes be avoided, but also, with careful planning, both
the LEP and mainstream students can profit from classroom
contact with each other.

Information About the
Students Facilitates Placement

In moving LEP students from structured English immersion (SEI) classes to the mainstream, school officials should examine the reports from the students' SEI teachers and any earlier school records. Discussions with parents and the students themselves can provide additional data. A person in the community who knows the child's language or a good translation service can help with this. From the interviews and reports, officials can find out to what extent the students have been taught literacy, mathematics, science, and other subjects in their native languages.

The only true commonality among LEP students is that their dominant language is a language other than English. Some LEP students may have the background to qualify for advanced and/or gifted programs. Other students may have learning disabilities or behavior problems that could easily be mistaken for language difficulties.

Success of an Extraordinary LEP Student

Some rare students may be similar to David Ho, a 12-year-old Chinese immigrant child who entered a central Los Angeles school in 1964 without any knowledge of English. With 6 months of ESL instruction and watching American television, David could get along in the language minimally. He soon showed himself to be skilled in math and science. Because there were no restrictions at the time that could have forced him into low-level classes until he had gained English proficiency, David participated in accelerated math and science classes. As a result, after graduation from high school, David was accepted into MIT and later Caltech. In 1996, David Ho became *Time* magazine's "Man of the Year" because his molecular biology research had led to incredible advancements in the fight against AIDS.

This is an unusual story, but it makes the point that each student must be evaluated carefully. Most LEP students in Grades K–8 will be able to enter a regular class within a year and, with some extra assistance, do perfectly well.

LEP STUDENTS CONTINUE TO RECEIVE HELP IN THE MAINSTREAM

Federal and state laws require that LEP students receive extra assistance until they measure close to grade level according to English language proficiency tests, standardized reading tests, and writing samples. That level is referred to as "reclassification" because students move from LEP to non-LEP status. The cutoff scores that separate LEP from non-LEP student status are based on state or national averages; thus, they can be lower or higher than the norms of a particular school. Very often, those scores will not agree with the cutoff points at which SEI and classroom teachers have agreed to move LEP students from SEI into the mainstream. That point is reached when the LEP students have enough fluency in English to get along in a mainstream classroom according to measures developed by the teachers at the individual school.

However, state and federal laws require that students who move from SEI to the mainstream continue to receive extra assistance as long as they are classified as LEP. To make this possible, schools can choose one or more of the following four options:

1. Classroom teachers gain special training through college or inservice courses.

2. A resource person provides inservice and in-class assistance to teachers new to teaching LEP students.

3. A resource room provides remedial assistance in a variety of ways.

4. Instructional aides are assigned to classes with LEP students.

ESL/Bilingual Education Endorsements. The special training must be in bilingual education or ESL courses. Generally, a teacher with 9 to 12 credit hours in these classes is considered qualified to work with several LEP students in a mainstream class—perhaps one LEP student for each 4 to 6 native speakers.

The Resource Teacher. A teacher with English language acquisition expertise, referred to here as the resource teacher, can become vital to classroom teachers who find themselves at a loss as to how to instruct LEP students. That teacher can be called on to present inservice training to groups of teachers who have a particular grade or subject area in common. The purpose would be to present information on LEP or ESL techniques and allow the teachers to develop their own strategies.

For example, the resource teacher may solicit suggestions from a group of third-grade teachers as to effective ways to use visuals. As the teachers respond with information based on personal experiences, the resource teacher takes their suggestions a step further by elaborating on ESL activities applicable to the teachers' ideas. Back and forth, the resource teacher and classroom teachers create and build on each other's experiences and knowledge.

In future sessions, the resource teacher can ask the mainstream teachers to discuss what they have found to work particularly well with their LEP students. In other words, the teachers share with each other while the resource teacher guides them along by using his or her own specialized knowledge.

In a school with a small LEP population, a trained SEI teacher may be divided between teaching SEI and resource work. This is beneficial in that the resource teacher has first-hand knowledge concerning what does and does not work in the classroom, with regard to the particular curricula at that school. Also, resource teachers who teach at least part-time in the classroom daily have increased credibility with classroom teachers.

The resource teacher should be available to meet with a classroom teacher as well as to demonstrate a strategy to a class while the classroom teacher looks on. The classroom teacher may have left out some detail in his or her presentation that has prevented the strategy from working as well as it could. By observing the resource teacher with his or her students, the classroom teacher learns what to do step-by-step.

The Resource Room. Some schools have created rooms that offer LEP students assistance through computer programs, instructional aides, and peer tutors. The person in charge may be the resource teacher or another professional. The students can be scheduled to visit the resource room during the school day or after school.

The resource room can serve as a means for students to work on their language skills. Computers can be used very effectively in this room. Information is available at the end of the chapter concerning *Rosetta Stone*, a popular CD-ROM program, and specific cost-free web sites that specialize in providing materials for LEP students.

The resource room can offer help on content area assignments. The teacher or aides can coordinate with the classroom teachers to make it possible for a group of LEP students to receive extra help on a lesson causing difficulty. Peer tutors can be trained to provide similar assistance. Like the instructional aides, peer tutors must be trained and directed by an experienced teacher of LEP children. Peer tutors should be chosen for having demonstrated maturity with classmates, good language skills, a willingness to be helpful, and responsibility.

Sometimes it is necessary for the teacher in charge of the resource room to offer lessons that deal with specific cultural differences. That might include aspects of shopping in stores, the rules of popular sports, gestures, culturally based cleanliness standards, proper American etiquette, and cultural taboos.

The Instructional Aide. Classroom teachers can be helped immensely by instructional aides. These paraprofessionals can assist with discipline, individual student problems, classroom activities, setting up the classroom, calling parents, and other aspects of teaching. During a lesson directed by the teacher, the instructional aide can observe the students to make sure that they are all on task. If a student misbehaves or appears to be upset, the instructional aide can take the student out of the room and deal with the problem apart from the other students. This not only allows for necessary, immediate assistance to a troubled child but also prevents an interruption to the learning process of the other students. During a writing or reading exercise, the instructional aide can relieve the responsibility of the teacher and increase the effectiveness of the lesson by working with either a group of students or one student with special needs. If the instructional aide is able to speak a native language of the students, he or she can call parents and provide occasional quick translations.

As time passes, the classroom teacher and instructional aide often develop a close relationship in which the teacher not only directs the aide but also listens to him or her for insight. Some children hesitate to share their difficulties with the classroom teacher, but will open up to an instructional aide who can then convey the information to the classroom teacher. The relationship between classroom teacher and instructional aide should be a growing partnership.

Preparation for Teaching LEP Students in the Mainstream Classroom

A teacher who has done a good job with mainstream students can be successful with LEP students after those students have reached appropriate levels of achievement in the SEI program. In fact, adjustments made for LEP children might improve the learning for all children. The teacher who wants to succeed with LEP children should make a conscious effort to do the following:

- Review teaching techniques that have proven effective.
- Provide easy access to important resources.
- Encourage LEP students to participate in all activities.

- Create time slots when students can receive extra help.
- Address problems due to students' unfamiliarity with the English language.

Review Techniques of Effective Instruction

Educators differ in their opinions concerning the best way to teach children. Some methods work better for some teachers and students than for others. That "best way" can range from hands-on activities to projects to systematic learning. However, few educators question the importance of some general techniques such as maintaining discipline in a classroom, involving students in a learning activity as soon as they walk in the door, teaching only one concept at a time, providing plenty of practice for a difficult concept, and testing for mastery before moving on. A review of effective instruction can help teachers to better instruct LEP children. Training by Madeline Hunter is recommended because it has been shown to improve the teaching of LEP children considerably. Information regarding the *Madeline Hunter Collection* can be found at the end of this chapter.

Provide Easy Access to Important Resources

Maps. The classroom must contain at least two large maps, one of the world and one of the United States. Students from foreign countries should be encouraged, sometimes with the assistance of the teacher, to show the other students where they come from on the map. Teachers can help LEP children gain a perspective of the world and this country if they remember to point to places on the maps as those areas are mentioned in literature or conversation.

Charts. After a particular concept has been mastered, it is handy to have reminders in the form of charts on the walls. The content of these charts can range from geometric designs to explain fractions to general rules of spelling and/or punctuation. LEP students should be encouraged to participate in the creation of these visuals.

Reference Books. Every classroom should provide grammar books, various types of dictionaries, and other reference books. A recommended list of these books can be found at the end of this chapter.

Audiovisual Aids. CD-ROMs and audiocassette tapes that come with texts make it possible for LEP students to review lessons. Many examples are offered at the end of Chapter 3.

Lessons can be scripted by the teacher, instructional aide, or student helper and then carefully recorded on an audio-cassette. The voice on the tape must be easy to understand. By using both the script and the matching audiocassette, the students both hear and read the lesson as many times as necessary. As a result, the LEP students improve their listening and reading skills as well as master the lessons.

Encourage LEP Students to Participate in All Activities

Prearranged Questions. LEP students are often too self-conscious to speak freely in front of their English-dominant peers. It helps to let LEP students know a day ahead of time that they will be called on to answer specific questions. This gives them a head start to practice and prepare to speak before the class.

It is important that the question be understood by the individual LEP student and within his or her ability to answer. Possibly, the teacher can offer the LEP students choices as to which questions they will answer. Gradually, as LEP students succeed in answering prearranged questions, they will become more comfortable speaking before the class and will actually volunteer to answer questions spontaneously.

Sharing Experiences and Knowledge. LEP students can be a source of fascinating information for the teacher(s) and other students. They should be encouraged to share experiences and knowledge that relate to the lessons at hand. The LEP students can talk about the foods of their native countries in a lesson on nutrition. This can lead to an analysis of the nutritional value of the diets of various cultures. Geography lessons can become real as LEP students describe their trips through various continents, countries, and/or cities to reach the United States. Discussions concerning language differences can lead to lessons on comparative linguistics, the development of languages throughout the world, and/or the linguistic patterns peculiar to English. LEP students may share ways they learned mathematical and/or scientific concepts in their native countries; such information may be helpful to teachers who want to improve their methods of delivery in those subjects.

As the LEP students become contributors to the class, the other students broaden their view of the world. From this sharing, all students gain knowledge while developing mutual respect and tolerance for cultural differences.

Extracurricular Activities. Effort must be made to encourage students to participate in all the opportunities that are offered at a school. The LEP students should mix as much as possible with the native speakers to increase fluency in English and to feel comfortable in their new environment. Sports, plays, musical groups, and school government provide this necessary integration. The teacher sets the groundwork by fostering friendships among students that are based on mutual interests rather than native language. The teacher can tell the students what extracurricular activities are available and ask for student volunteers to accompany the LEP students to the activities.

The LEP students can compete on a par with other students in chess, checkers, and most sports. Most likely, the LEP students would enjoy teaching their classmates games and sports that are popular in their native countries. Plays that involve the LEP students' culture(s) can inspire the LEP students to participate in drama and to feel appreciated by the other students.

Native Language Development. If several students share the same language, lessons in that language can be taught to all the students. It would be a reversal of the usual format in that the LEP students would be the ones to assist the English-dominant students. Developing a foreign language program at the elementary level will be discussed in Chapter 6.

Create Time Slots When Students Can Receive Special Help

Remedial Assistance. There should be a time during the school day in which students can be provided extra assistance. Speech therapists, psychologists, reading specialists, LEP resource teachers, and other experts should be able to work with individual students without those students having to miss important lessons. The other students can work on advanced projects, read books of their choice, play educational games, and/or create new visuals for the teacher.

Homework Clubs. Some teachers begin assigning homework in the early grades whereas others encourage the students to read books at home rather than complete homework assignments. After-school homework clubs can provide opportunities for LEP students to work together on an assignment, review a lesson, and read aloud to each other. A teacher or other adult should supervise this activity.

Address Problems Due to Unfamiliarity With English

Simplify the Language. It is not uncommon for LEP children to have strange gaps in their English vocabulary. To facilitate understanding, the teacher can state the same thing a second time by using different words:

- "Who wants to participate? Who wants to do it?"
- "You must review the lesson entirely. You must study all of it."
- "That is not acceptable behavior. You must not act like that."
- "Pay attention. Listen to me."
- "Complete the questions at the end of the chapter. Look at the questions on Page 5. Write down the answers to the questions."

Diction and Speed. Sometimes an LEP student needs to hear something spoken at a slightly slower pace and with clearer diction than usual. Also, the teacher should pause for an additional second at the end of a sentence or where a comma would be inserted to allow LEP students time to process what has just been communicated.

Visual Aids. It is important for the teachers to write assignments and directions on the board. They should use gestures, expressions, and visuals to get across a concept. As teachers make explanations, they can assist LEP students by drawing primitive pictures on the board, such as a point that stands for "sharp," a circle to designate "around" or "surrounding," or traditional lines to signify "greater than" or "less than."

Student Helpers. It is not a good idea to put LEP children next to students who speak their native language. The result will be a great deal of translating that encourages dependency on the native language. Of course, in some instances there is no choice but to call on students who can explain concepts in the native language. However, most of the time, it makes sense to put an LEP child next to a student who does not know the native language of the LEP student, but who enjoys being helpful. Students who tend to daydream may become more attentive if they know that they are expected to relay a lesson to LEP classmates.

The non-LEP students learn to summarize by rephrasing to LEP students what has just been explained by the teacher or read in a text while LEP students profit from hearing their fellow students' explanations. For socialization and to make sure all students have the chance to summarize, the students' seating assignments should be changed often.

Assignment Buddies. Frequently, LEP students do not understand homework assignments or directions, but are not inclined to speak up about it. A way to handle this problem is to have students divide into pairs, or "buddies." After the teacher has written the information on the board, instructed the students to write it down, and then given them enough time to do so, he or she can ask the students to check if their "buddies" have actually followed the instructions. The teacher instructs the students to raise their hands only if their buddies do not have the work written down, so that the teacher can come to help out. This way the students who missed the activity are made aware of what they are supposed to do without embarrassment.

Actual Objects. All students remember the names of objects best after they have seen and touched them. The teacher should take time to pass around elements essential to a lesson such as wooden or plastic objects that can be in the shape of spheres, squares, triangles, octagons, and so on.

Frequent Checks. When LEP students are asked in front of class-mates whether they understand a concept, they often claim that they understand when they don't. Thus, teachers should give frequent short quizzes on specific topics that the students know they must prepare for. It is unreasonable to expect LEP students to study or be able to take tests on a large amount of material that has not been taught thoroughly in small segments.

By engaging the students in informal conversation, the teacher can get an idea as to how much material the students have grasped. For this to be productive, the teacher should avoid asking "yes" and "no" questions. It would be better to say "Show me how you got this answer" and "What step did you do first?" If students are unable to respond, it may be necessary to offer them choices such as, "Did you divide, multiply, or something else?"

Outlining Daily Activities. As already mentioned in previous chapters, the LEP students need to know what to expect. The teacher should write on the blackboard the goal of a lesson, such as "We are going to learn how to write fractions," or "We are going to read about the U.S. Constitution." If possible, a schedule should be kept on the board throughout the day. All of the day's activities should be arranged in sequence.

Providing Alternative Assignments. Because students just out of SEI classes are likely to have some difficulties with communication, it may be practical to allow these students to demonstrate their knowledge of a subject through visuals. The students can prepare a *PowerPoint*™ demonstration on the computer, discuss an activity such as a visit to the zoo with video shots or photographs, or use pictures to tell a story. Also, the visuals help the other students to understand those students who are still struggling with the language.

Evaluating Student Progress. The goal in grading students' work is to provide feedback that makes it possible for the students to improve. Handing back papers without corrections or papers that are filled with red marks from beginning to end are extremes that should be avoided. Also, a student should never be graded down for not knowing what he or she has not been taught.

LEP students will make blatant language errors because they are still in the process of internalizing the basics of the English language. Common mistakes include "He talks English" rather than "He speaks English," or "I have 9 years" rather than "I am 9 years old." One solution is to write down and later record the correct phrases on individual audiocassettes for the students to practice.

The grade should only reflect how well the students prepared the assignment and demonstrated what was taught. Sometimes it works to count two or three mistakes of an LEP student as equal to one mistake of a native English speaker.

Pantomimes With Storytelling. As the teacher reads a story aloud, student volunteers can silently act it out. When the teacher reads, "Martha was unhappy because her friends laughed at her," a student acting the part of Martha makes a sad face while the others appear to be jeering.

Teaching Vocabulary Systematically. It is very helpful for the teacher to provide opportunities for the students to master the major vocabulary in a lesson before actually beginning that lesson. This can be done by means of charts, the blackboard, or handouts. Words should be divided into word groups. The following is an example of word groups for a science lesson:

Nouns		Adjectives	Verbs
drift	vapor	invisible	to cling
glacier	molecule	rough	to splash
clearing	particle	tiny	to spray
icecap	temperature	solid	to sink
iceberg	chunk	liquid	to stretch

The students should be supplied with a list of definitions and examples of how each word can be used in a sentence. After going over the list, the teacher can begin asking questions:

- "What is the difference between a glacier and an iceberg?"
- "What is an example of something that can be described as a 'chunk'?"
- "What is the difference between something solid and something liquid?"
- "If you touched a glacier, would it feel solid or liquid? Explain."

The students can draw pictures that will help them visualize and remember the words. They can play games to guess the words and then be encouraged to create their own sentences. From that, they can write their own questions. By taking time in these ways to introduce the vocabulary, teachers will discover that students are able to read a lesson more easily.

Latin and Greek Roots. Like English, the native languages of LEP students frequently consist of words derived from the Latin and Greek languages. From the third grade on, students can learn to relate words in their native languages to words considered difficult in English by becoming aware of word roots. This develops into a learning tool for all students.

Example: Increasing Vocabulary. Mr. Matias, a fifth-grade teacher, shows the students the Latin root "bene" on a large index card. He explains that the word is Latin for "good" and then asks whether the students know a word in another language that is similar to "bene" that means "good." Marco, a Spanish-speaking student, replies "bueno" and another student says "bien." Daniel, a Rumanian boy, identifies a word in his language. Mr. Matias then writes down words with "bene" under the appropriate headings on the board. He says the words and then the students repeat them:

Nouns	Adjectives	Verbs
benefit	beneficial	to benefit
benefactor	benign	
benevolence	benevolent	
benediction		

Next, Mr. Matias shows the students the "mal" word root card and asks if anyone knows its meaning. If no one volunteers the answer, he explains that it means "bad" and then writes "mal" words down under the same headings:

malady	malicious	to malign
malformation	malignant	
malevolence	malevolent	
malediction		

Mr. Matias assigns students to look up one or two of these words in the dictionary, define them, and use them in sentences. The students write their work on the board. Mr. Matias goes over each word with all the students. He erases everything but the words, makes up his own definitions, and challenges the students to figure out which words he is asking for:

- ■ "The birds are flying out of order. We say that they are flying in . . ."
- ■ "What do we call someone who gives away money or something valuable?"

- "When something helps us, we say it is . . ."
- "Benediction means 'blessing,' something you say to wish something good for someone or something. What would be the word for 'curse,' something you say to wish something bad for someone or something?"

Mr. Matias encourages the students to find additional words in the dictionary with the "bene" and "mal" word roots. He warns them to check to be sure that their roots actually mean "good" or "bad."

Over the following days, Mr. Matias does similar exercises with other combinations:

uni- (one)   magn- (large)   nox-, noct- (night)   mascul- (man)
du- (two)   min- (little)   dia- (day)   femin- (woman)

Finally, Mr. Matias reviews the word roots by showing the cards one at a time with the roots written on them and then encouraging the students to think of the English words that contain those roots. After the students say the words, Mr. Matias writes the words on the board and prompts the students to identify those words. A book on word roots can help with this activity; one is recommended at the end of this chapter.

Idioms and Slang. Native speakers of English use idioms and slang more frequently than they realize. For instance, the phrases "stick one's neck out," "four-letter word," "clown around," and "put the heat on" are found in everyday conversation and cause no confusion to native speakers. However, to LEP students, they can be quite misleading. The LEP students must have these phrases explained to them and then be allowed to practice them.

Example: Fun With Literal Meaning. Mr. Matias asks for a volunteer to explain the phrase "The man got fired from his job," when it appears in a story.

A boy named Paul asserts, "The man lost his job."

Mr. Matias replies, "That's right, but you just used an idiom to explain an idiom. Try again, Paul, and be more literal."

Paul says, "The man had a job until he was told he couldn't work there anymore."

Mr. Matias writes down the idioms and Paul's translation of them for the students to copy.

Mr. Matias asks LEP student Sonya, "Why do you think that the man was fired from his job?"

Sonya answers, "He was fired because he didn't do the work, or maybe there wasn't enough work."

Mr. Matias asks Kenji, another LEP student, "What is another reason that the man may have lost his job?"

Kenji replies, "He lost his job because he came to work late."

Learning idioms and slang can become an enjoyable activity. Some students may want to draw pictures of phrases that depict both their idiomatic and literal meanings. Students who are native speakers become more aware of their language by having to explain it to new English learners while the new English learners learn common expressions. A book series of American slang and idioms is listed at the end of this chapter.

Grammar Through Writing

Students will likely forget grammar rules unless they have opportunities to practice the rules as soon as they are learned. This process can begin as a group activity in which, ideally, only one LEP student is assigned to a group of three or four.

Example: More Complex Sentence Combining. Fourth-grade teacher Ms. Kahlo asks the students to tell her everything they remember about Frederick Douglass, a person they have studied in a recent history lesson. As the students provide information, Ms. Kahlo writes it down. She purposely puts the words in the usual columns that divide them into nouns, adjectives, and verbs:

runaway slave	famous	was able to speak up in 1841
companion to boy	handsome	saw his mother only at night
African American	very smart	was whipped by his master
fighter for rights	courageous	fought to free slaves

She asks the students to put together complete sentences. Students offer the following: "Frederick Douglass was a runaway slave because he was whipped by his master" and "He was an African American and fought to free slaves."

Ms. Kahlo asks them to complete the following:

"Frederick Douglass was a runaway slave who . . ."

A student replies, "was whipped by his master."

She shows them how they can put more information about Frederick Douglass into the sentence: "Frederick Douglass, an African American, was a runaway slave who was whipped by his master."

She asks the students to give other examples of words to put between the commas. They answer, "Frederick Douglass, a very smart man," "Frederick Douglass, a courageous African American," and "Frederick Douglass, a fighter for rights."

In groups of three, the students put together paragraphs of three or four sentences about Frederick Douglass. They must use the new structure, nouns in apposition, at least twice. After Ms. Kahlo has collected the papers, she evaluates the paragraphs for accuracy and organization. She puts the best examples on the board and discusses those short paragraphs with the students. Likewise, she talks about the other paragraphs one at a time by pointing out the paragraphs' strengths and weaknesses. She encourages students to come up with ways to improve the paragraphs.

On the following day, Ms. Kahlo follows the same format of writing information on the board. Students are now providing information concerning another historical character about whom they have recently read. On this day, the students work in pairs. On the third day of this lesson, the students write paragraphs individually about yet another familiar, famous person. This activity is continued until students have mastered the art of using nouns in apposition in their writing.

This sentence-combining technique can be applied to teaching students how to insert all types of clauses into their writing. It can become a game to see who can put the most information into a single sentence. Most important, the students become interested in and adept at writing sentences and paragraphs while learning content.

DRAMA AS A TOOL FOR IMPROVING ALL ASPECTS OF LANGUAGE

Children like to play make-believe and to take on the roles of various characters. From the earliest grades, LEP students can participate in the process of creating and performing a play. Through developing the story line, writing down the action and words for each part, and then performing the play, the LEP students practice hearing, speaking, reading, and writing the English language authentically. These steps suggest a format:

1. *Choose the subject.* The play can be a dramatization of a historical event or any fictional work such as a scene in a novel, a short story, a nursery rhyme, a poem, or something created by the students themselves. The teacher guides the students into establishing the action of the play and then dividing it into acts and scenes.

2. *Roles.* Students and teacher brainstorm to figure out how to make sure each student has a speaking part in the play. The play may have to include a chorus of speakers and/or several narrators to explain the details of what happens between scenes.

3. *Write the acts and scenes.* This is the organizational phase of the activity. The class divides into groups of three to four students, with each group writing a specific scene or act. The students of each group should offer suggestions and agree with the final format.

4. *Proofread each section.* The groups pass their work to other groups who go through the writing and make suggestions. The writing can be passed around as many times as necessary to produce good, sequential versions.

5. *Use a word processor to type out the final drafts.* Depending on their age, the students can either type out the various sections of the play or turn the work over to the teacher, an aide, or older students.

6. *Review the play.* The students read the final product orally and in sections. They can suggest changes after the reading has been completed. It is important that they notice consistency as the play progresses and that each scene and act leads appropriately into the next.

7. *Assign roles.* Students volunteer for parts. Everyone must speak either individually or in a group.

8. *Provide for props, costumes, and scenes.* Just how elaborate this becomes depends on what is available and how much time the teacher wants to devote to it. Students may be able to bring in clothing and objects to make the play appear more real.

9. *Practice the lines.* At this point, students can record themselves to practice diction and pronunciation. Students help each other to ensure that the lines can be understood.

10. *Perform the play.* The end product can be a play recorded on an audiocassette, a video dramatization, or an actual performance in front of another class.

PROBLEMS THAT MUST BE ADDRESSED

Whereas conditions are seldom ideal for teaching LEP students, they should always be reasonably good. Sometimes it is necessary to compromise or improvise; other times, large changes must be made. If students are not learning for reasons that become obvious to the teachers, those teachers must speak out. A few of the most common problems are the following:

■ *Placed too early into the mainstream.* Students who cannot speak English should not be put into the mainstream until those children have been instructed for approximately one year in SEI. The SEI and mainstream teachers should decide the criteria and adjust them periodically. Students placed too early into a mainstream class may become frustrated. All the students in the class may suffer because of the extra burden put on the teacher.

■ *Placed too late into the mainstream.* Students should not be held back in the SEI class if their oral language skills measure up to the criteria set by the teachers. Students who have difficulty with literacy should be helped through a remedial program available to all students with literacy problems.

■ *Unreasonable number of students in the mainstream classroom.* A class of 20 students, of which 5 are classified as LEP, is a class of reasonable size whereas a class of 30, with 10 classified as LEP, is unreasonable. A possible solution would be to provide a well-trained instructional aide and/or other helpers. There are no absolute rules or guidelines for this, but each school must find a reasonable balance.

■ *Bad acoustics.* It is crucial that the LEP students be taught in rooms where disruptive noise is minimal. This eliminates classrooms next to gyms, choir rooms, or busy highways. It means that the heating system and air-conditioners are reasonably quiet.

■ *Lack of materials.* There are many ways to compromise, such as using materials found on the Internet or at home. However, it is important for the teachers to make requests for whatever they believe would contribute to their instruction.

SELECTED RESOURCES FOR TEACHERS

Computer Programs for Improving Linguistic Ability

- *The Rosetta Stone Language Library* (1-800-788-0822 or www.RosettaStone.com) is a CD-ROM program that allows students in Grades 1 through 12 to work independently on vocabulary building, grammar, spelling, punctuation, and even pronunciation.
- *Activities for ESL Students* at http://a4esl.org/ and *Selected Links for ESL & EFL Students* at http://www. aitech.ac.jp/~iteslj/ESL.html are cost-free web sites that provide practice sheets that deal with vocabulary building, American idioms, geography, homonyms, all aspects of grammar, reports, and other topics through a quiz format.

Professional Help

- *The Madeline Hunter Collection* consists of 11 separate books that offer suggestions for increasing effectiveness in the classroom. Each book can be obtained through Corwin Press (1-805-499-9774 or www.corwinpress.com).

Reference Materials

- *The Basic Newbury House Dictionary of American English* by Heinle & Heinle (1-877-633-3375 or www.heinle.com) is designed as a combination picture and word dictionary. This 15,000-word reference book offers expanded definitions for 2,500 words, 750 illustrations, maps, encyclopedic information, and irregular verb charts.
- *Dictionary of American Slang* by HarperCollins (www. harpercollins.com) can be purchased at www.amazon. com or in leading bookstores such as Barnes and Nobel, Borders, and Crown. The third edition of this book is regarded as the standard for American idioms with its more than 19,000 terms; it has been updated to keep up

with new developments in technology and the global economy.

- *English Vocabulary Quick Reference: A Comprehensive Dictionary Arranged by Word Roots* is written by Roger S. Crutchfield and published by LexaDyne Publishing (1-888-599-4700 or www.quickreference.com/).

- *The Oxford Picture Dictionary for the Content Areas* for elementary and middle school LEP students is published by The Oxford University Press (1-800-451-7556 or www.oup-usa.org/esl/). This book presents over 1,500 vocabulary words as illustrations from social studies, history, science, and math with 60 topics put into eight units to accompany mainstream core curriculum.

- *Understanding and Using English Grammar* is written by Betty Schrampfer Azar and published by Prentice Hall (1-800-382-3419 or corpsales@pearsontechgroup.com). This book offers comprehensive explanations of all fundamental rules of grammar, complete with examples and exercises.

Slang and Idiom Series

- *The Street Talk series*, available through Optima Books (1-800-515-8737 or www.optimabooks.com/), presents common American slang and idioms in small paperbacks. They offer amusing dialogs that place idioms beside their literal meanings.

6

Fostering
Student
Achievement
Through
Whole-School
Programs

The limited English proficient (LEP) children must achieve at a much faster rate than the non-LEP students if the LEP children are ever to catch up to the mainstream children academically. This requires careful, deliberate instruction of the most essential information in each content area, as indicated throughout this book. Also, LEP students must be assessed frequently to guarantee that they are progressing satisfactorily.

Besides establishing a deliberate, frequently reexamined academic program for LEP children, other improvements that involve the entire school should be considered as well. These include academically focused early childhood education, extended time in school, programs for parents, involvement with the elderly, effective attendance policies, alignment of the curricula, and language instruction in the LEP students' native language.

Every school culture has its own particular characteristics and problems. Also, each school must work within boundaries of money and space constraints. Thus, it is essential to choose courses of action that bring about the highest level of achievement for the greatest number of students at that school. Ideas can be put forth, but only the administrators and teachers who work with the children daily can judge what will be most useful to their particular school. Schools, to be effective, must determine which one to three priorities will be the subject(s) of focus. To make many areas "priorities" is to dilute the effort and accomplish little.

The following suggestions are an accumulation of what successful school administrators and teachers have recommended as essential to the improved achievement of LEP children in their respective schools.

ALL-DAY PRESCHOOL AND/OR KINDERGARTEN

All-day preschool and/or kindergarten allows LEP children the opportunity to catch up early to the native English-speaking children. Successful school superintendents from districts with high numbers of LEP children in Arizona and Texas have stated that the one factor that made the greatest difference in improving LEP students' achievement has been early childhood education. The instruction must be based on definite curricula that include phoneme awareness, early language development, and numbers. Each teacher should be fully trained to instruct these children in groups of reasonable size, generally classes of 15 to 25 students, with the assistance of a full-time instructional aide.

The LEP children should enjoy this experience and not feel pressured in any way. Montessori schools have been successful in teaching small children for decades with a discovery approach in which the children are guided to move from one skill to the next at their own pace. A recent study of Georgia's preschool/kindergarten (pre-K) programs indicates that early age lessons that take into account the children's natural interests can ensure that they do well later on as learners in the primary grades (Thompson & O'Quinn, 2001, p. 1).

Initially, due to the school budget, a school may only be able to offer all-day kindergarten to at-risk students. After the achievement of these at-risk students has increased, less money will be needed for remedial programs later on. The saved funds can then be used for half-day preschool. When that has proven effective, the next step would be to provide all-day preschool and, in time, to fund the early childhood education programs for the mainstream students as well. Gradually, this process can lead to the optimal situation in which 3- to 5-year-old LEP children spend the entire day learning with their native English-speaking peers.

YEAR-ROUND SCHOOL

Year-round school keeps LEP students from losing their English language gains, as frequently occurs when students are away from English for several weeks at a time. Instead of a 3-month summer break, the students take 6 weeks off for summer with 2- to 3-week vacations divided into three intervals that are spaced evenly throughout the school year. During the 6-week break, students should be given some work to take home—perhaps some high-interest reading materials. The 2- to 3-week vacations make it possible for schools to establish intersessions that provide remedial catch-up instruction, additional English language development, and/or other academically related activities. Many teachers welcome the opportunity to earn additional money for their intersession instruction; also, it is easier to find volunteers to help for short rather than long time periods.

EXTENDED-DAY SCHEDULING

Extended-day scheduling makes it possible for LEP students to participate in homework clubs, tutoring, computer programs, and various other activities that require them to understand and speak English. It is important to note that school is sometimes the only place where these children can study because of crowded home situations. Sometimes it is crucial for schools to stay open during early evening hours not only to offer activities but also to serve as a haven for children who would otherwise be left home alone or who would be in homes where there is no quiet place to study.

INVOLVEMENT OF PARENTS

Involvement of parents produces a bond between the parents and the school. This takes effort on the part of the school authorities because many parents of LEP children are embarrassed to come to school because they know either limited or no English or have received little schooling themselves. Also, the parents often work long hours that do not correspond to the school day. Newsletters, home visits, and telephone conversations in the native language alleviate these problems somewhat, but are usually not enough.

Back-to-school nights, when parents have the opportunity to become acquainted with teachers, are helpful, but often produce disappointing turnouts because the LEP children tend to keep the information about the programs from their parents. These children fear that their parents will learn something negative about them from their teachers. Putting each child in charge of the presentation to his or her parent can prevent this. That way, the child is able to show off his or her accomplishments. Discussing a student's progress can be designated at a separate time or over the telephone. Also, providing food, a festive atmosphere that relates to the minority culture(s), and performances by LEP children may help to draw good crowds on those special nights. Having speakers of the language visit neighborhood associations, churches, and other organizations as school representatives may increase parental visits to school as well.

The parents of LEP children often want to learn English and will take advantage of opportunities to do so. This was proven when Proposition 227 in California mandated that English instruction be offered at the schools for LEP adults. The English classes became so popular that the governor of the state decided to increase the funding for them. This has led to classes for parents to learn how to help their children with homework and basic reading skills. In some cases, it has meant that parents learn alongside their children.

The main purpose is to draw as many parents of the students to the school as possible and then to encourage the parents to become participants in their children's education.

RELATIONSHIPS WITH THE ELDERLY

Relationships with the elderly offer LEP children the chance to become appreciative of older people while practicing English. A weekly visit from a group of LEP children to a senior citizen center can lead to meaningful one-to-one relationships between children and English-speaking seniors. The elderly tend to speak slowly and clearly; thus, children have an easier time communicating with them than with people of other age groups. The elderly and the children can read books to each other and then discuss them. Many older citizens enjoy working with young people. This can lead to positive results for both groups.

INCENTIVES FOR EXCELLENT ATTENDANCE

Incentives for excellent attendance provide reasons for students to attend school regularly. At a Washington, D.C., conference on literacy, a principal explained how, in the migrant community of Dover, Florida, the Dover Elementary School authorities had decided that they had to improve attendance if they were to increase the rate of achievement of the mostly

LEP students. As a result, they developed a chauffeur service to pick up students who had missed the bus or been delayed for some other reason. Also, through funding from business partners, staff members, the Parent-Teacher Association (PTA), the community, and grants, the Dover school began to offer rewards for perfect attendance that included special pins, savings bonds, parties, pep rallies, attendance extrava-ganzas, and days at the Busch Gardens amusement park. Now Dover Elementary leads all the schools in Hillsborough County in average daily attendance (Carr & Dickerson, 2001).

In some states, such as Texas, the state law is very strict concerning school attendance. Parents can be fined heavily and be forced to attend school with their children for several days if a court of law establishes that their children have missed school for indefensible reasons.

ALIGNMENT OF THE CURRICULA

Alignment of the curricula brings about continuity of instruc-tion for all students. This lessens the possibility of duplication of material and mandates that students focus on specific skills and content. Some states provide this alignment through state standards that work especially well for the many LEP students who move within a state. Some basic agreement among states for specific national standards could further assist the LEP children whose parents' jobs take them from state to state.

One argument against standards is that they force teachers and students to put a great deal of their time into lessons that are not interesting to them. The solution is for the standards to be reasonable and to offer flexibility as to how they are taught. The students should have the opportunity to learn what is most essential in ways that are appealing. For this to be done, states must make the effort to consult classroom teachers and allow them to participate in the process of developing good standards that they can support wholeheartedly. As with all instruction, review and modification of standards should be an ongoing process.

To support state standards and/or to develop continuity of learning in schools where the states have not yet established specific standards, programs that promote sequential instruction are available. The Core Knowledge Foundation content, for instance, provides 50% or more of the content to be used for a school's curriculum. The school can then supply some of its own preferred content and skills to complete the curriculum. Direct Instruction offers scripted lessons that build on skills with frequent assessments that make it unlikely that any time in the children's education will be wasted. Both programs are discussed further in the following paragraphs. Contact information is provided at the end of the chapter.

THE CORE KNOWLEDGE FOUNDATION

The Core Knowledge Foundation, founded by E. D. Hirsch, Jr., developed K–8 content guidelines after a long process that involved noted educators and specialists, as is noted in *Core Knowledge Sequence: Content Guidelines for Grades K–8* (Core Knowledge Foundation, 1998). This group analyzed reports from state departments of education and professional organizations such as the National Council of Teachers of Mathematics and the American Association for the Advancement of Science. They looked at the successful educational systems of other countries such as France, Japan, Sweden, and Germany. The foundation's advisory board made suggestions regarding content that encompassed relevant diverse cultural traditions. After several revisions, a master list was created from which additional groups of teachers and specialists decided on a grade-by-grade sequence of items in the areas of language arts, history, geography, mathematics, science, and the fine arts.

DIRECT INSTRUCTION

Direct instruction can be found in Advantage Schools (for-profit charter schools) that operate in eight states and the

District of Columbia. These schools have a highly structured program that works especially well for new English language learners and other at-risk students. Students learn in small instructional groups based on academic skill level rather than grade and are assessed on each skill before moving on to the next. Aides as well as teachers can be trained to present the scripted lessons.

Each lesson builds on previously mastered skills that have been field-tested and devised so that 90% of the students grasp a lesson the first time around. The content areas include reading, language arts, spelling, mathematics, and science.

INSTRUCTION IN LANGUAGES OTHER THAN ENGLISH

Instruction in languages other than English makes it possible for bilingual students to build on their knowledge of their home language(s) and for native English speakers to learn a new language. Knowledge and proficiency in more than one language can benefit children as they enter into a global world where good communication is essential for increasing cooperation and trade among nations.

The LEP children should measure up to the norm of their English-speaking peers in listening and speaking skills before taking on any instruction in languages other than English. In other words, students in structured English immersion (SEI) classes do not qualify for this instruction at first.

However, after the LEP children have moved beyond SEI and totally into the mainstream classes, they may participate with the other children in brief (20- to 50-minute) lessons in languages other than English. If the focused language is the children's native language, their participation should depend on various factors. For some children, it may be a useless experience to sit through basic conversation lessons of a language that they know fluently; for other children, especially very young children, it may be the highlight of their day to be able to learn specific information such as the days of the week or how to count in their native language. Of course, this is a wonderful opportunity for an advanced or former LEP student to help native speakers of English learn a foreign language. As literacy in the new language is introduced, all students should be encouraged to participate.

From the language surveys filled out by the parents on the day of enrollment, school officials have obtained information as to which children in the school have been exposed to languages other than English. They can contact the parents of these children to find out if they want their children to develop oral language skills and literacy in the primary language or a different one. It should not be taken for granted that the parents would want their children to study the primary language. For instance, Vietnamese parents may request that their children learn Spanish or Japanese because those languages are spoken by a much larger percentage of the world population than is Vietnamese.

It makes sense to inquire whether a family member fluent in the particular language would be willing to help with its instruction. Even if that person comes in for only 1 hour once a week, it enables children to practice conversing with a native speaker. Also, encouraging family members to contribute is a way to improve relations between the school and the home.

Once it is established that the parents would like their children to study a language other than English, it is up to the school authorities and parents to make decisions concerning which language or languages will be implemented and to what degree. There are many ways to implement the study of a language other than English. Immersion similar to SEI offers the most effective methodology, whether the time allotted to the study is short (20 minutes a day) or extensive (50-90 minutes a day). With large populations of LEP students, it may be advisable to offer classes for native speakers of that language that are separate, at least for some of the time, from those for non-native speakers of that language.

■ *After hours.* Additional classes can be arranged through community education services for LEP students to continue to learn their native languages and cultures. Because these classes are offered before or after school, in the evening, or on Saturday, it is often not necessary for a certified teacher to instruct them. People who have never taught should receive some instruction in techniques and routines.

■ *20 minutes in primary school that builds to 50 minutes in Grades 4 to 8.* In a school with a high number of LEP students, it is unwise for these students to spend more than a minimal amount of the school day on a language other than English because the emphasis must be on English language development and literacy. Approximately 20 minutes total in the primary grades is enough time for all students to learn basic vocabulary and become familiar with the grammar. This segment should have its own curriculum composed of objectives and outcome assessments with the lessons integrated into the other curricula as much as possible. For instance, the objectives to learn numbers and colors in the new language can be combined with the instruction of arithmetic and art. By fourth grade, it should be possible to introduce literature in the new language and to continue to align the new language curriculum with the other subjects in various ways.

■ *50 minutes in primary school that either remains at 50 minutes or builds to 90 minutes in Grades 4 to 8.* This would be appropriate at a school that focuses on the development of a language other than English as an important part of its curriculum. Ideally, the population of the school should be stable rather than mobile, because this instruction assumes that students will be in the same school for at least one full year. Parents must be willing to commit to making sure that their children do their homework. This requires serious language study that should not be expected of students with oral language and/or literacy deficits in English.

■ *Equal time divided between two languages, commonly referred to as dual-language.* This requires students to gain as much knowledge in two languages as they would if they learned exclusively in English. It also works best for a stable school population and requires commitment from parents.

Because of the intensity of instruction that this program demands, it is inappropriate for students who score below the 75th percentile in reading, language, and/or math on standardized tests in English. The schools must have the option to admit into the program only newly enrolled students who test at academic levels equal to those of the dual-language students and to transfer students who fall behind into classes where most of the instruction is in English.

Information regarding programs that offer audiovisual aids that can be used to assist with the study of languages other than English can be found at the end of this chapter.

Principles to Build On

For a school to be successful with LEP students, certain points should be considered:

- The earlier the age that the school immerses LEP children in English, the greater is the likelihood that they will catch up academically to their English-speaking peers.
- Various programs before and after school as well as throughout the year provide LEP children additional opportunities to increase their English language proficiency.
- Parents of LEP children who are encouraged to come to school for a variety of reasons are likely to become involved in their children's education.
- One-to-one contact with the elderly allows LEP children the chance to practice English in an enjoyable and non-threatening way.
- Incentives, especially in farm communities, may be necessary to encourage LEP children to come to school daily.
- Skills taught systematically and content that is aligned result in academic success, particularly for LEP children.

- Languages other than English can be taught most effectively if integrated with the other subject areas whenever possible.
- Respect should always be shown toward the primary language; opportunities should be presented for the children to continue study in that or other languages if the parents desire it.

SELECTED RESOURCES FOR TEACHERS

Whole-School Programs

- *Core Knowledge Sequence* at the Core Knowledge Foundation (1-804-977-7550 or www.coreknowledge.org).
- *Direct Instruction* at Advantage Schools (1-888-388-9012 or www.advantage-schools.com).

Foreign Language

- *Rosetta Stone* (1-800-788-0822 or www.RosettaStone.com) offers programs on CD-ROMs that make it possible for K–12 students to choose among at least 23 different languages. Language books, workbooks, study guides, quizzes and tests, handbooks for teachers, and activity books are included.
- *2000 World Languages* by National Textbook Company (1-800-323-4900 or www.ntc-school.com) offers complete programs for the K–8 study of Spanish, French, German, Italian, Russian, and Japanese. Materials include texts, workbooks, various reading books, teacher's manuals, dictionaries, CD-ROMs, videotapes, audiocassettes, flashcards, posters, song/story transcripts, and hand puppets. This company has available additional materials for the older children in Grades 9 through 12 who want to study Spanish literature or additional languages such as Vietnamese, Malay, Indonesian, Polish, Swedish, and Hindi.

7

Structured
English
Immersion
Essentials

A Brief Review

Structured English immersion (SEI) makes it possible for children whose dominant language is not English to become successful in the mainstream as quickly as possible. The previous chapters detail the following processes that are necessary for this to happen:

1. Identification of the limited English proficient (LEP) students who need this program

2. Placement of LEP students

3. Instruction that prepares students for the mainstream

4. Timely transition into the mainstream

5. Mainstream classroom strategies particularly helpful to LEP students

6. Whole-school programs that encourage LEP students to achieve

This chapter summarizes these steps.

IDENTIFICATION OF LEP STUDENTS

All parents answer questions on a survey about their children's language(s) so the school officials can determine whether these children should be administered oral language proficiency tests in both English and the home language. Also, teachers are expected to refer, for the same testing, those students who appear to be having difficulty in their classes because their dominant language is not English.

As established by the language surveys completed by parents or by teacher observation, the following criterion is the only reason that a student should be administered the oral language proficiency tests:

■ The child has difficulty with English because the child can communicate in another language better than in English.

Other criteria *do not qualify* as reasons for administering the oral proficiency exams:

■ The child has difficulty communicating, but knows only English.
■ The child can speak another language, but communicates better in English.

INITIAL PLACEMENT OF LEP STUDENTS IN ACCORDANCE WITH TEST RESULTS

After students have been administered the oral language proficiency tests and it has been established that their dominant language is not English, their score results determine whether they should go into SEI classes, receive special services as transitional LEP students in the mainstream, or be totally mainstreamed as students who are proficient in English. The flowchart shown in Figure 7.1, based on the IDEA Proficiency Test (IPT) and Language Assessment Scales (LAS) publishers' recommendations, suggests how to do that.

ADVANCING THROUGH THE LEVELS

Before students move on to the next level, it is best to use teacher-prepared tests singly or in combination with an English language oral proficiency exam. Whenever there is a conflict between test score results, the teacher-prepared test and other teacher/parent observations should be given more credibility that the English language oral proficiency exam.

There are various choices available for students who have completed SEI 1, 2, or 3. The teachers should decide the criteria for each and be willing to have students repeat or skip levels when appropriate. Figure 7.2 (see p. 113) shows the sequence from SEI 1 to the mainstream.

SEI INSTRUCTION

The SEI levels have been divided into three sections. SEI Level 1 is the beginning entry level for those students in Grades K–6 who have little or no understanding of English. This level concentrates on getting students started with the language through a structured format. SEI Level 2 is for students in the second and third grades; SEI Level 3, for those in the fourth grade and above. SEI 2 and 3 students continue to work on listening comprehension and improving oral skills while moving into the content areas—where they develop their literacy skills in a systematic way.

SEI 1 Format	SEI 2 and 3 Formats
Listening emphasized through TPR	Continued TPR in modified forms

Figure 7.1   Placement of Students According to Oral English
Language Proficiency Tests

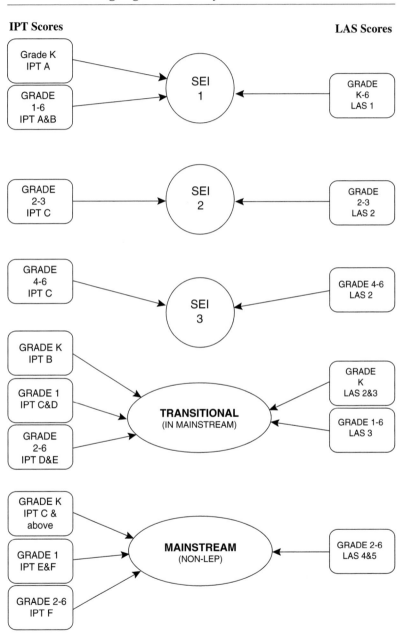

Figure 7.2   SEI Level 1 to Mainstream Sequence

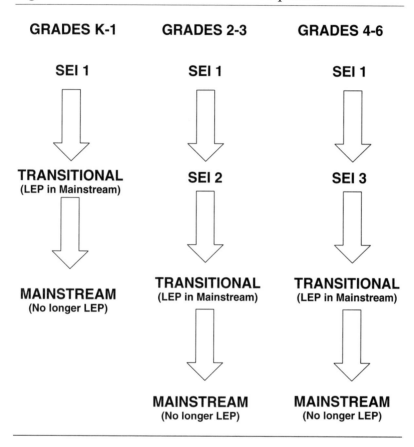

Everyday conversation   Content aligned with mainstream
Short oral responses   Formation of questions, orally
                             and written

Basic grammar   Grammar as a tool for literacy
Occasional written work   Daily written work
Mainstream contact   Mainstream contact gradually
  limited   increased

Activities for All SEI Levels

■ Role play, sometimes in skits, that can be enhanced with
   props and costumes.

- Listen to stories from teacher, cassettes, and/or CD-ROMs.
- Describe pictures and objects.
- Write short dictations.
- Respond to "Simon Says" type formats through movement or short replies.
- Identify letters and words through "Hangman" type games.
- Review information such as colors, pets, and numbers through team competitions.
- Repeat poems and chants to improve pronunciation, intonation, and inflection.

Activities Specifically for SEI Levels 2 and 3

- Read aloud in unison with class and as "echo" to teacher.
- Read reciprocally aloud with a partner, or make predictions and create questions about a paragraph both children have read silently.
- Write daily in journals.
- Take dictations based on content.
- Retell and summarize content information, both orally and in writing.
- Look at unidentified students' work critically and offer suggestions for revision.
- Combine sentences to express information more succinctly.

TIME IT TAKES TO TRANSITION INTO MAINSTREAM

Kindergarten and First Grade. Depending on the students and the school, the students at these ages can frequently be mainstreamed from the beginning. However, it occasionally may be necessary to spend extra time on particular skills or to create activities to ease the transition from the structure of the native language to that of English. With larger LEP populations or in schools where the regular classes are at higher than usual achievement levels, these students should move through SEI 1 fairly rapidly (2 to 5 months) and then into the mainstream with possibly some continuation of LEP transitional services.

Grades 2 Through 6. Most students will need to spend a full school year in SEI classes, first in SEI 1 and then in SEI 2 or SEI 3. Some students will have to repeat a level—which could mean that they would spend 1½ school years in SEI classes. It is possible, but unusual, for students who start at SEI 1 to be able to exit the SEI classes in less than one school year.

Transitional. Students may qualify indefinitely for additional assistance in listening, speaking, reading, and writing skills. State laws generally require that students must score within 10 points of the norm of their grade level in each of these areas to be reclassified (i.e., to no longer be eligible for extra services).

MAINSTREAM CLASSROOM STRATEGIES

Teachers can adjust their instruction to LEP children in ways that enhance learning for all students. This can be done in a variety of ways:

1. Students' knowledge and understanding of each other are increased by their sharing of cultural experiences.

2. By serving as models for students who are learning the LEP students' native language(s), the LEP students receive affirmation for their native language while the native speakers of English are helped to learn a foreign language.

3. Native speakers learn to summarize by explaining lessons to LEP students who, at the same time, profit from their peers' explanations.

4. Students are taught in ways that support a variety of learning styles.

5. Students learn more easily because lessons are presented systematically, with clear communication, and often by means of audiovisual aids.

6. Students are kept on track as a result of frequent assessments.

WHOLE-SCHOOL PROGRAMS THAT ENCOURAGE LEP STUDENTS TO ACHIEVE

The following school programs are particularly effective for LEP students:

1. All-day preschool and kindergarten that include instruction based on academic curricula.

2. Year-round school with vacations spaced evenly so that students can spend intersessions catching up and other instruction can be offered.

3. Extended-day scheduling that provides several opportunities for students to practice and develop their English.

4. Involvement of parents, which breaks through language/ cultural barriers.

5. Relationships with the elderly that profit both children and seniors.

6. Incentives for students to come to school every day.

7. Curricula alignment that lessens the possibility of duplication and makes sure that students gain essential knowledge.

8. Instruction in the students' native language or another one of choice.

Resource A

Recommended Reading for Practitioners

Books and Articles

Asher, J. J. (2000). *Learning another language through actions.* Los Gatos, California: Sky Oaks Productions.

This is the fifth edition of Dr. Asher's 1977 book that explains the rationale and methodology of Total Physical Response (TPR).

Baker, K. (1998). Structured English immersion: Breakthrough in teaching limited English proficient students. *Phi Delta Kappan, 80*(3), 199-204. Bloomington, Indiana: Phi Delta Kappa International.

Baker builds a convincing case for the superiority of structured English immersion (SEI) over bilingual education.

Brownlee, S. (1998, June 15). Baby talk. *U.S. News & World Report, 124*(3), 48-55. New York: U.S. News & World Report.

This article tells how Johns Hopkins linguists have reached the conclusion that children's ability to learn a language peaks at age 6.

Carter, S. C. (2000). *No excuses: Lessons from 21 high-performing high-poverty schools.* Washington, DC: The Heritage Foundation.

This small book profiles and analyzes 21 successful schools, many with high numbers of limited English proficient (LEP) students.

Center for Equal Opportunity. (Ed.). (2000). *The ABC's of English immersion: A teachers' guide.* Washington, DC: Center for Equal Opportunity.

This 44-page collection of articles provides research, methodology, and other pertinent information on the subject of SEI.

Day, E. M., & Shapson, S. M. (1996). *Studies in immersion education* (pp. 5-40, 86-99). Clevedon, Philadelphia, & Adelaide: Multilingual Matters.

In three chapters of this book, the authors discuss studies of French immersion programs in Canada that indicate immersion students' grammatical deficiencies can be remedied if their French language instruction includes a focus on systematic grammar.

Eckman, F. R., Highland, D., Lee, P. W., Milleham, J., & Weber, R. R. (Eds.). (1995). *Second language acquisition theory and pedagogy* (pp. 131-185). Mahwah, NJ, and Have, UK: Lawrence Erlbaum.

Researchers show that the explicit teaching of grammar would improve immersion education.

English as a Second Language (ESL) and Bilingual Education Study Committee. (1999, November 17). *Arizona State Legislature minutes of meeting.* www.azleg.state.az.us/iminute/house/eslbil1117.doc.htm

Some of the foremost experts in both bilingual education and SEI meet with Arizona politicians to debate various topics such as how LEP children should be identified and how long it should take before they are mainstreamed.

Glenn, C. L., & de Jong, E. J. (1996). Educating immigrant children: Schools and language minorities in twelve nations. *Garland Reference Library of Social Science, 921.* New York: Garland.

Glenn and his colleague have put together a complete study of how twelve countries of Western Europe have developed public policies to minimize difficulties and increase educational opportunities for their many immigrant and refugee children.

Hirsch, E. D., Jr. (1996). *The schools we need and why we don't have them* (pp. 17-42). New York: Doubleday.

This chapter explains how we have failed disadvantaged children in our schools and how other countries have been able to close the achievement gap.

Lapkin, S. (Ed.). (1998). *French second language education in Canada: Empirical studies.* Toronto, ON, Canada, and Buffalo, NY: University of Toronto Press.

These studies were completed by researchers throughout Canada who used the most current research methodologies to offer in-depth analyses of French acquisition programs in their country.

Lapkin, S., & Lotherington, H. (Eds.). *The Canadian modern language review.* Toronto, ON, Canada: University of Toronto Press.

This journal presents the latest research and reviews of recent books on the various subjects related to the acquisition of modern language(s).

Palincsar, A., David, Y., & Brown, A. (1992). *Using reciprocal teaching in the classroom: A guide for teachers.* University of California at Berkley: Brown/Campione Research Group.

This manual offers teachers extensive directions and variations for using reciprocal teaching (RT) in the classroom. A videotape is also available for this purpose.

Porter, R. (Ed.). *READ perspectives.* Washington, DC: READ Institute.

This periodical presents recent research and discussions by experts regarding various aspects of English language acquisition programs in schools throughout the United States.

Roderick, M. (2000). Hispanics and education. In Pastora San Juan Cafferty & David W. Engstrom (Eds.), *Hispanics in the United States* (pp. 123-174). New Brunswick, NJ: Transaction.

This article examines and interprets the data concerning the education of Hispanics in this country.

Rossell, C. (2002). *Dismantling bilingual education, implementing English immersion: The California initiative.* Public Policy Institute of California: San Francisco.

This 105-page report offers in-depth analyses and recommendations concerning the implementation of California Proposition 227 into the English language acquisition programs of California.

Useful Web Sites

Educational Testing Service Network at www.ets.org

English for the Children at www.onenation.org

Eric Clearinghouse on Languages and Linguistics at www.cal.org/ericcll

Lexington Institute at www.lexingtoninstitute.org/education

National Center for Education Statistics at www.nces.ed.gov

National Clearinghouse for Bilingual Education at www.ncbe.gwu.edu

Public Agenda Online at www.publicagenda.org

Research in English Acquisition and Development (READ) Institute at www.ceousa.org/READ

Resource B

Exemplary Structured English Immersion Programs

No school exists that includes everything that I have recommended in this book. However, many schools and entire school districts throughout the United States have successfully implemented their own structured English immersion (SEI) programs. Below is a list of some of those schools and districts as well as the names of contact persons.

Arizona

Alhambra Elementary School District
4510 N. 37th Ave.
Phoenix, AZ 85019
602-336-2920
Federal Programs Director

Glendale High School
6216 W. Glendale Ave.
Phoenix, AZ 85301
623-435-6200
Principal

Nogales Unified School District
310 W. Plum Street
Nogales, AZ 85621
520-287-0800
Federal Programs Director

Phoenix Advantage Charter School
3738 N. 16th St.
Phoenix, AZ 85016

602-263-8777
Director

Thunderbird High School
1750 W. Thunderbird Rd.
Phoenix, AZ 85023
623-915-8900
Principal

Arkansas

Portland Elementary School
314 Highway 278 East
Portland, AK 71663
870-737-4333
Principal

California

Atwater Elem. School District
1401 Broadway Ave.
Atwater, CA 95301
209-357-6100
Superintendent

Bennett-Kew Elementary School
11710 Cherry Ave.
Inglewood, CA 90303
310-680-5400
Principal

Kelso Elementary School
809 E. Kelso St.
Inglewood, CA 90301
310-419-2526
Principal

*Oceanside Unified School
District*
211 Mission Ave.
Oceanside, CA 92054
760-757-2560
Superintendent

*Orange Unified School
District*
1401 N. Handy
Orange, CA 92867
714-628-4163
English Language
Development
Coordinator

*Riverdale Unified School
District*
3086 W. Mount Whitney
P.O. Box 1058
Riverdale, CA 93656
559-867-8200
Superintendent or
Asst. Superintendent

Florida

Dover Elementary School
3035 Nelson Ave.
Dover, FL 33527
813-757-9457
Principal

Pennsylvania

*Bethlehem Area School
District*
1516 Sycamore St.
Bethlehem, PA 18017
610-807-5599
Superintendent

Texas

Kipp Academy
7120 Beechnut
Houston, TX 77074
713-541-2561
Principal

Glossary

Bilingual education Description of an instructional program that utilizes two languages, one of which is English. The student learns in a language other than English, usually the student's native language, at the same time that the student learns English.

ESL (English as a second language) Students are instructed in the use of the English language. The instruction may or may not involve use of the native language and is taught during specific school periods.

FEP (fluent English proficient) The level at which a student scores proficient in English language listening and speaking skills.

IPT (Idea Proficiency Test) A popular test by Ballard & Tighe for measuring the English proficiency of students whose native language is not English. It has an oral, a reading, and a writing section. The commonly used oral portion of the IPT must be administered one-to-one and usually takes from 5 to 20 minutes.

LAS (Language Assessment Scales) A popular test by CTB McGraw-Hill for measuring the English proficiency of students whose native language is not English. It has an oral, a reading, and a writing section. The commonly used oral portion of the LAS must be administered one-to-one and usually takes from 10 to 15 minutes.

LEP (limited English proficient) The term used by the federal government, most states, and local school districts to identify those students who have insufficient English skills to succeed in English-only classrooms without extra assistance. Recently, the term ELL (English language learner) has come into favor with many educators as a replacement for LEP.

NAEP (National Assessment of Education Programs) Standardized-test-score interpretations that have been conducted regularly by the U.S. Department of Education since the early 1970s. These assessments of 9-, 13-, and 17-year-old students in the areas of mathematics, reading, science, writing, history, and geography examine trends in skill levels according to race and ethnic groups.

OCR (Office of Civil Rights) A U.S. Department of Education agency that investigates school programs to make sure that they comply with federal civil rights requirements.

PHLOTE (primary home language other than English) The designation given to students who have been identified through a language survey as understanding and speaking a language other than English.

SAE (standard American English) The English language that is used and accepted as correct in the United States.

SEI (structured English immersion) The methodology in which LEP children are taught English through English immersion with little or no reliance on the native language. Students learn English through structured and sequential lessons that are specially developed for LEP students and based, to a large degree, on the mainstream curricula.

TPR (total physical response) A second language/foreign language methodology developed by James J. Asher in the late 1970s in which students develop listening skills in the target language by responding physically to commands.

Transitional LEP The level beyond SEI when LEP students have been fully mainstreamed but still qualify for extra assistance.

References

Amselle, J. (1996). The failure of bilingual education. *Index of Bilingual Education Statistics* (pp. 111-123). Washington, DC: Center for Equal Opportunity.

Amselle, J., & Allison, A. C. (2000). Two years of success: An analysis of California test scores after proposition 227. *READ Institute.* Retrieved January 2002, from http://www.ceousa.org/READ/227rep.html

Annual Surveys of the States' Limited English Proficient Students and Available Educational Programs and Services. (2000, October). Rural districts struggle to serve new populations. *Bilingual Education Report,* 1-6.

Brownlee, S. (1998, June 15). Baby talk. *U.S. News & World Report,* 48-55.

Carr, K., & Dickerson, L. (2001, October 9). *The ABCs of literacy.* Handout at Leadership for Literacy: Leverage Points for Policymakers, Education Testing Service Conference, Washington, DC.

Carter, C. (2000). *No excuses: Lessons from 21 high-performing, high-poverty schools.* Washington, DC: Heritage Foundation.

Center for Equal Opportunity. (2000). *The ABC's of English immersion: A teachers' guide* (pp. 38-40). Washington, DC.

Clark, K. (2000). From primary language instruction to English immersion: How five California districts made the switch. In *Educating language minority children. READ abstracts* (Vol. 6, pp. 146-175). New Brunswick, NJ: Transaction.

Core Knowledge Foundation. (1998). *Core knowledge sequence: Content guidelines for Grades K–8* (8th ed.). Charlottesville, VA: Core Knowledge Foundation.

Crawford, J. (1997). The campaign against Proposition 227: A post mortem. *Bilingual Research Journal, 21*(1), 1-27.

Day, E. M., & Shapson, S. M. (1996). *Studies in immersion education.* Clevedon, UK: Multilingual Matters.

English as a Second Language (ESL) and Bilingual Education Study Committee. (1999, November 17). *Arizona state legislature minutes of meeting.* Retrieved November 2001, from http://www.azleg.state.az.us/iminute/house/eslbil1117.doc.htm

Federal gov't must do more for Hispanic ed, study says. (2000). *Bilingual Education Report, 1*(3), 1-7.

Fitzgerald, J. (1995). English as a second language learners' cognitive processes: A review of research in the United States. *Review of Educational Research, 65,* 145-190.

Harley, B., Howard, J., & Hard, D. (1998). Grammar in grade 2: An instructional experiment in primary French immersion. In S. Lapkin (Ed.), *French second language education in Canada: Empirical studies* (pp. 177-193). Toronto: University of Toronto Press.

Krashen, S. D., & Terrell, T. D. (2000). *The natural approach: Language acquisition in the classroom* (3rd ed.). Essex, UK: Pearson Education.

Larsen-Freeman, D. (1995). On the teaching and learning of grammar: Challenging the myths. In F. R. Eckman, D. Highland, P. W. Lee, J. Milleham, & R. R. Weber (Eds.), *Second language acquisition theory and pedagogy* (pp. 151-167). Mahmah, NJ: Lawrence Erlbaum.

Lightbown, P. M., Halter, R. H., White, J. L., & Horst, M. (2002). Comprehension-based learning: The limits of "do it yourself." *Canadian Modern Language Review, 58*(3), 427-464.

Morris, L., & Tremblay, M. (2002, March). The impact of attending to unstressed words on the acquisition of written grammatical morphology by French-speaking ESL students. *Canadian Modern Language Review, 58*(3), 364-385.

Proposition 203. (2000, November 7). State of Arizona Ballot Propositions & Judicial Performance, General Election.

Rossell, C. (1999). Mystery on the bilingual express: A critique of the Thomas Collier study. *READ Perspectives, 5*(2), 5-32.

Rural districts struggle to serve new populations. (2000). *Bilingual Education Report, Best Practices, Assessment and Legislative News, 1*(2), 1-6.

Steinberg, J. (2000, August 20). Increase in test scores counters dire forecasts for bilingual ban. *New York Times,* Front Page.

Thompson, C., & O'Quinn, S. D. (June, 2001). Eliminating the black–white achievement gap. *First in America,* p. 1.

Index